For The Deranged Lunatic In All Of Us

So You Want To Be An Extremist

A Motley Manifesto for the Motivated Maniac

C.T. Jackson

Contents

Welcome, Future Illuminatus

"People Love Conspiracy Theories."

— Neil Armstrong, Professional
Actor

L ife is tough, isn't it? You work hard and try your best,
but in the end you are stuck, sitting there in the fading
light in your underwear with this bright yellow book in
your hand. Something seems to always be getting in the way of
your professional or personal success. Maybe you are facing a full-
blown existential crisis, brimming with anxiety about a world
that you can no longer understand or control as the years slip by
faster and faster while the once comforting aspects of life crack
and crumble and the meaningless void becomes darker and
bigger, threatening to envelop everything you believe in and
everyone you know. Or maybe you are just bored or something.

Now you are here, wondering who to blame. You have picked
the right book. This guide will help you hone your abilities to
uncover the real truths about your failures. Your lack of success is
not because you are an incompetent, lazy dolt. No, it is due to a

secret cabal of elitist, lizard people who have been plotting against you for decades.

It is time for you to join the ranks of the needlessly skeptical, but that does not mean you have to live in a tinfoil house. No, in fact, the world of extremism has become increasingly normalized. It is full of schemes, pills, potions, podcasts, and even politics. This world is ripe for exploitation if you properly understand and embrace it. This book will show you how to do both. And you don't even have to put on pants. In fact, it is better if you don't.

OVERVIEW OF THIS GUIDE

This guide is divided into three main sections. Each section requires you to reject more and more of reality until your brain has reached the pinnacle of deranged enlightenment – an extremist nirvana. By the end of this book, you shall have ascended to the 5th dimension or at least convinced yourself and others that you have. Most importantly, you will be able to grift plenty of followers out of cash to pay for your ascension. The higher planes of existence aren't cheap, after all.

The first section provides you with a comprehensive history of truth, how it was concealed by those in power, and how others who came before you uncovered it. It will then focus on providing you with the means to tear down the false walls of reality that have prevented you from achieving your absolute potential. This includes learning how to reject facts, observations, and experience and instead, embrace what you *feel*. That is where the real truths lie – right below the upper intestine.

The second section teaches you how to build out your image as an all-seeing eye of truth. This includes how to dress appropriately, what tools you need to showcase yourself in your new reality, and how to build out and advertise your new ideology for others to follow. Tinfoil hats may help you avoid the government from reading what little is left of your brain, but they tend not to attract others to your cause. At the very least, don't use the generic brand of tinfoil.

You will also need to master the new tools that theorists of today use to spread their messages. The days of forwarding chain emails are over, Grandpa. Social media is the new conduit of contradiction. It is where realizations are found in 10-second videos, where the lowliest Reddit comment can become the greatest uncovering of truth, and where beliefs become facts within a few hundred characters.

Next, embrace outrage. The angrier you are about a new conspiracy you discovered, the angrier your followers will become and the less they will question actual facts about your ideology. In that same vein, always question everything. Rhetoric – and thus – rhetorical questions are part of your fiber now. These lessons will come in handy in the later part of this guide as you work toward becoming something more than just a personality or ideology.

The third and final section focuses on how you can capitalize on your newfound character. There are dozens of social, political, and environmental crises that are ripe for exploitation. Make no mistake, whatever crisis you choose, those in power are behind it. They are likely planning something even more sinister. You must work to expose them to the masses, and if you can make a few dollars off of it, then why not? You need that capital to finance more in-depth investigations such as half-assed Google searches and frequenting 4chan threads. Those degenerates always have their finger on the pulse.

How can others learn about you and your quest for the truth if there isn't anything to buy and tell them about it? Writing blogs and yelling at people with a megaphone on the street are good ways to get the people to pull their heads out of the sand. However, selling them t-shirts is another way to get the message out. Selling questionable supplements will ensure that they have the energy to keep digging for the truth. Hosting a podcast with advertisers can also help boost the range of your messaging.

Once you have cultivated a strong following of other truth-seekers, you can begin to elevate your own worth as their leader. You are the one who has seen behind the curtain, gazed upon the Great Oz, and comprehended the objective truths of the universe. You should be powerful. You should be praised. That is the final step for the extremist. The ultimate extreme. Thus, this book concludes with understanding this final state of being, this last truth. Perhaps, you will find conspiracy nirvana by the time you reach the end of this guide. Let's not get ahead of ourselves though. The journey to profundity begins with a single question. Who are you?

SOVEREIGN CITIZEN

You are self-made. You do not need any government handouts like welfare, roads, healthcare, police, or firefighters. In fact, you don't need the government at all. You may reside in the geographical area of the shadow government, but you don't adhere to its laws or principles. You are your own citizen of You-a-stan. It is the shadow government that is actively trying to prevent you from living a life of ultimate, unabashed freedom. Why should you have to pay taxes on your barbed wired compound in Western Idaho? You built it with your own two hands. That money would just go to the evil leaders and their child sex trafficking rings. How disgusting. You married your 12-year-old niece and her sister because of freedom. Just as the Bible, God, and the Constitution intended. Isn't it time you learned how to fight back against these socialist, federal Nazis? So, polish that AR-15 and read on.

MODERN LIFESTYLE GURUS

You made the right choice in buying and reading this book. Even if you had to cut back on your monthly amethyst enema purchase. It is a worthy sacrifice, and your horoscope said it would be beneficial. Well, it wasn't lying, mercury is in retrograde after all. Whatever that means.

You have learned not to trust authority in any situation, whether it be medical, political, financial, or social. It is all run by old white men and their jackbooted stormtroopers trying to turn tomorrow into 1984. They won't stop you though, not with your chamomile oil, sapphire crystal necklace, and a degree in sociology that you have from that online college.

If the people and authorities could just align their chakras, then everyone can live happily ever after and pick berries in upstate Vermont. If only everyone would listen. Well, with this book, they will. So, take a swig of your acai lavender detox tea and read on.

ARMCHAIR SCIENTISTS

Dr. Anthony Fauci may have retired from government, but his reign of terror lives on. And you have been fighting for years on the front lines against him and the bloodthirsty 5G vampires that run the Centers for Disease Control (CDC). You have seen through the false veil of peer-reviewed medical science. The government tried to control you and your family with their mind-control-laden vaccines, but you would not give in or back down.

You are resilient, like untreated measles or syphilis. Doctors are nothing but charlatans and government stooges in white coats, paid by the rich elite to experiment on you and your children with antibiotics, x-rays, and sound medical advice. You know who else wore white coats? The Nazis. Well, probably. Like when they went to an evening ball or a fancy dinner. Not you though, you know the truth. Go ahead and put Dr. Oz on pause, get that Ivermectin ready, and read on.

SOCIAL MEDIA CONNOISSEURS

Feel free to take breaks during this section every few seconds so you can scroll through all of your social media apps. Lies move fast and you need to constantly stay on top of them to avoid being duped by your enemies and your friends. Plus, you don't want to miss the new prank video from that 15-year TikTok influencer.

For you, the truth is in the hands of the people and in their hands are their phones. The geriatric generations who run the secret governments are trying to keep you dumb and docile. You know better, because you are doing that by yourself. You and your online echo chamber colleagues are out there (not literally) asking questions, challenging the status quo, and tirelessly working toward connecting the dots of seemingly unconnected events and people. You see the patterns that are not really there. Or are they? Keep asking those questions and read on.

YOUNG WHITE MALES

Welcome, Generation Z, you are finally old enough to make decisions, exercise your right to vote, and participate in the economy. You really fucked all of that up, didn't you? Not that the previous generations did any better. You are part of the new broligarchy. You are the raging, hormone-filled response to the Diversity, Equity, and Inclusion (DEI) millennials who came before you. The rest of the world seemingly blames you for everything, yet you know better. You listen to the wise sages of Joe Rogan, Theo Von, Ben Shapiro, Charlie Kirk, and numerous others via podcast. All the while you sit in your basement inner sanctum, trading crypto and trolling liberals on X.

You somehow believe in everything and nothing simultaneously. Everything is a joke until it is about you. No more. You may sit in the red-capped shadows, but you can see that the evils of the world are being perpetrated by the "libs." It is time you take back what you never owned by creating your own extremist movement and riding to right-wing Valhalla. Pop some creatine pills and continue reading.

Whether you see yourself in these categories or not, whomever you are, you all have many things in common. You, and those like you, probably don't test high on cognitive ability, but that stuff is just a way for the government to control how you think by – in this case – making you think. People may often classify you as suffering from overly narcissistic behavior, but in reality, you just have a lot of self-love. That is healthy. When they call you a religious or spiritual whack-a-doo, yet again, they are simply jealous that you can see things on a higher plane of existence, which they will never experience.

You are not burdened with facts and figures, you don't speak from the brain, you speak from the gut and shoot from the hip. This guide will keep you well fed and well-armed to take on the malevolent machinations, conspiring corporatists, and sinister Deep States seeking world domination. Rise up and read on, fellow truther!

Converse meaningfully with fellow humans and neighbours...

Publish everywhere immediately now

Comments 21

Most Relevant ↓↑

 **DefinitelyYourFellowCitizen96** ✓ 4 seconds ago

fuck you and fuck all of yr opninon. i am tpying at the speed of brain and i calculate many different understanding

41,423
Re-Shits

CHAPTER 1

FROM FIRST TO ICONOCLAST

"History is a set of lies agreed upon."

— NAPOLEON BONAPARTE, BATTLE OF
WATERLOO RUNNER-UP

To fight the future, you must understand the past. This chapter is dedicated to learning about the history of lies, theories, and truth. History is often written by the victors, but this isn't about that. Instead, let's look at a collection of the past's conspiracies and why the victors were actually ancient aliens. It is time for you to take back history, just as you will take back the future.

THE FIRST STEP

First, there are two key definitions you need to know for the rest of this book and their relationship to each other. The world of extremism is vast. Thus, we must set boundaries on what is possible to be covered in the following pages. The main focus of this guide is how the psychology of alternative thinking is often a starting point to accepting more radical and fringe beliefs. This is the more gradual road to extremism that you will explore. Other types of radicalization occur from catalyst events or nationalistic grievances that springboard people into more extremist circles rather quickly. After all, there is only so much time you have on this flat earth after all, so focus on what you can.

Live Life To The Extreme

Let's define our first term – EXTREMIST. It is important to know what this means as you will be working toward it throughout the course of this book.

In the simplest of terms, extremists are far too sure of their opinions on everything. They hold steady regardless of the facts presented. They tend to be entrenched in their beliefs even if they are wrong – and they will never admit they are wrong. Extremism has roots in politics, but the definition can be expanded to all areas of society, brought on by an increase of echo chambers in social media, a drop in critical thinking skills, and a rise in conspiracy theories to explain an ever-more complicated world. Extremists often reject the cultural, political, and social norms of the state. They are intolerant of others' beliefs; they eschew democracy as a governing system and generally disavow the entirety of the social order they are a part of. Extremists are just really great people with whom to spark a deep conversation. They definitely won't yell and go crazy on you after a few minutes. The two greatest enemies of an extremist are reason and acceptance. You will learn to hate those ideas as well, if you haven't already started before picking up this book – which was likely the last reasonable thing you will do. It is time to forget that those terms exist and start your slide down toward one end of the social spectrum. It is like finding the end of a rainbow, but instead of a pot of gold, you will find a pot of hate, confusion, and insanity. Faith and begorrah!

A (Conspiracy) Theory of Everything

In its most basic definition, a conspiracy theory is the belief that a secretive group is responsible for a tragic, harmful, or even heroic event. The conspiracy theory has been used by people for hundreds of years to make sense of a complex and complicated world. While this belief has been around for centuries, this current definition was solidified in the zeitgeist after the events of September 11, 2001. This is when George W. Bush flew two planes into the World Trade Center towers. When terrible events happen, people want simple answers. It is actually comforting to those who believe in these theories. Why? Well, because if there isn't a cabal of rich evil men then it would mean the world is chaotic, uncontrollable, and unpredictable. This is far scarier because there is no concrete person or thing to blame, it's nebulous. The unknown and the uncontrollable are terrifying compared to a few old rich people in power. A conspiracy theory is like a thick blanket, it comforts you, but it can also smother you. You might be into that, though, and that is fine too.

Let's now take a brief step back into history to learn about the conspiracy theories and the extremists who trailblazed the path for future generations of insanity like you.

When in Rome

Ancient Rome, one of the longest lasting and greatest civilizations in history, had a lot of strange beliefs. Whether it was using urine to clean their clothes, drinking gladiator blood to cure epilepsy, or thinking that unibrows were attractive, the Romans were far from strait-laced. So, it comes as no surprise that they came to believe a conspiracy theory or two. The most famous one concerns the death of Emperor Nero (AD 37 – AD 68). You may know Nero from the story of how he played the fiddle (he was really into Bluegrass music) while Rome burned. This story is actually false, but who cares? Nero had plenty of crazy behaviors without needing any made-up stories. He murdered two of his wives – kicking a pregnant one to death – as well as killing his own mother. To be fair, she had taken away his fiddle and put him in time out. He couldn't let that slide.

Nero committed suicide in AD 68...or did he? Rumors began to emerge he had faked his death and was still alive in hiding, plotting to retake his throne. Others thought that he had died but was going to come back from the dead and take back his reign over Rome. To add fuel to the fire of these rumors, fake Neros began to pop up for the next several decades claiming their right to the throne. Soon, everyone in Rome would be playing fiddles.

A JEW IN KING ARTHUR'S COURT

From antiquity, we move to Medieval Times™, where your family gets dinner and a show! Wait, sorry that is the wrong Medieval Times. Also known as the Middle Ages, this 1,000-year span between 450 AD and 1450 AD spawned many a good conspiracy theory.

What would a good conspiracy theory be if it wasn't accusing the Jewish people of something horrible. This is where that time-honored tradition blossomed. One catalyst was the First Crusade around 1100 AD. This was the height of Catholic fanaticism as tens of thousands of unwashed Europeans, led by William II, marched toward Jerusalem to take back what they claimed was theirs from the Turks. The Turks responded with "finders keepers, losers weepers." While bloodshed was occurring a world away, conspiracy theories about the Jews were popping up across Western Europe. Just as the Catholics saw the Turks as enemies of Christ from afar, they saw the Jews as enemies of their savior, enemies right in their own backyard.

The term "Blood Libel" is the theory that Jews gather Christian children and sacrifice them on Easter to help in the baking of matzo (unleavened) bread. It does feel like there are easier ways to make bread, Who hasn't received a breadmaker as a present that they inevitably returned the next day? While the theory has roots in the first century BC, it became a popular conspiracy theory during the First Crusade. Within another century, the Church would adopt it as dogma, excluding Jews from the better part of

Christian society. They even made them dress differently to single them out daily. They were forced to wear parachute pants and neon t-shirts.

During this time, the artistic depictions of Jews evolved based on this conspiracy theory. By the early 1300s, frescos and paintings had Jews depicted with crooked noses, yellow skin, and demonic-like features. These were the precursors to how the Jews in Nazi Germany of the 1930s and Nazi America of the 2020s were portrayed by more modern Christian nationalists. The rich, covetous Jew trope started at this time and has continued through today.

TEMPLAR TEMPTATION

The Knights Templar was a group of soldiers that formed in early 1100 AD with the charge of protecting Christendom. They were instrumental in the Crusades as much as they were in banking – most of the over 15,000 members were very rich. They are often described as one of the first multinational corporations. Just like multinationals today, they did not pay any taxes. A popular conspiracy associated with the Templars was that they guarded the Holy Grail, the cup that Jesus Christ drank from that provides healing powers. This theory proved true when Indiana Jones found it in the desert some 700 years later.

For two centuries, the Knights were essential to Christian Europe. Once the Crusades ended in late 1291 AD, they found themselves without a purpose. They had reached their midlife crisis. So, while some went out and bought a Porsche and dyed their hair, the majority of the group found themselves targeted by the French king, Philip IV.

Figure 1: An Historian's Reconstruction of the Knights Templar's Holy Grail

On Friday the 13th in 1307, King Philip put on a Jason hockey mask and ordered the mass arrest of members of the Knights Templar. He mostly wanted to seize their vast wealth. He promoted a number of conspiracy theories to justify these raids. In his decree, it was mentioned that the Templars had been engaging in sodomy, pederasty, Satanic worship, sorcery, hunting without a license, hunting with a license, jaywalking without a license, and illegally downloading Metallica albums. Several of the leaders were burned at the stake and the order was disbanded.

Many of the remaining members would go on to found other secret organizations – most notably, the Freemasons. So, they leaned even further into the conspiracy theory lore. Rumors continued after the disbandment of the Templars concerning a vast hidden fortune of treasure that they had hidden. Thankfully, Tom Hanks found it a few centuries later.

Enlight It Up

After the darkness of the Middle Ages came an intellectual and philosophical movement known as the Enlightenment. This period between the late 17th century and the end of the 18th century gave society new ideas on science, philosophy, medicine, government, and better ways to fold a burrito so it doesn't make a huge mess when you bite into it and then the beans shoot out the front and now you have to turn it around and eat that side to avoid it getting worse, but that doesn't work so well because you now have it open on both sides and it is just a goddamn mess.

It also gave birth to new secret organizations and conspiracy theories to go with them. Probably one of – if not the most – famous secret organizations was founded at this time. In the mid-1700s, Adam Weishaupt founded the Illuminati in Bavaria, Germany (there were early groups in France, Italy, and Spain that used the nomenclature, but the Bavarian Illuminati is most similar to the group discussed in modern times). Their goal was to combat the role of religion and its influence on public life, which it deemed an exceedingly abusive exercise of government and state power. The irony of course is that the conspiracy theories about the Illuminati claim they were doing that behind closed doors.

The Illuminati were outlawed a few decades after being formed, brought on by support from the Catholic Church and influential conservative citizens. They are often blamed for the French Revolution. This would be one of the first events – but not the last – that the group would be accused of orchestrating. Today, the group is associated with the "New World Order," being even more shadowy and able to control all major events, wars, economic downturns, the reason you never win at Monopoly, the Chicago Cubs winning the World Series, assassinations of famous leaders, Nicholas Cage movies about the Declaration of Independence, and a host of other activities. It seems they are always busy.

JACOB'S LADDER

Another secretive group worth mentioning operated at the same time as the Illuminati. They were known as the Jacobins because all the members were named Jacob, which made it hard to assign duties. Regardless, conspiracy theories have labeled them as a radical group who ushered in the French Revolution (everyone wants to take credit for it). In fact, they emerged at the start of the Revolution, and helped finish that "Ancien Regime" off. They pushed for purges of their opponents and were linked to foreign states and wealthy donors who wanted to see the upheaval of France. Sound familiar? Like January 6th familiar? They were directly responsible for the "Reign of Terror" that followed the Revolution, where opponents were tried and executed by guillotine – or worse – by being forced to watch Jennifer Lopez's *Gigli* repeatedly.

X MARX THE SPOT

In the 1930s, a far-right antisemitic (the Jewish people never get a break) movement emerged in Nazi Germany known as Cultural Bolshevism, named after the socialist movement in the Soviet

Union. In the early 1990s, this movement reinvented itself in the United States and was known as Cultural Marxism. These postwar German philosophers were known as the "Frankfurt School." This term is often parroted on Fox News as the beginning of the end of American society. The conspiracy theory it was built on posited that a small cadre of Jewish philosophers fled Germany as the Nazis were gaining power and set up in Columbia University in New York City. They were planning to upend American culture, society, and the economy. According to the conspiracy theory, these Jewish philosophers – most notably Herbet Marcuse (who all the 1960s leftist kids loved to quote) – were planning to convince the American public that being proud of your white ethnic heritage was bad, that Christian "family values" were bigoted, and that everyone should engage in and accept some level of sexual liberation. Honestly, that all sounds pretty good. However, to the less-than-open minds of Americans in the 1990s, it might as well have been the equivalent to sacrificing children during Easter for unleavened bread. But can you blame the public? It was so long ago; they didn't know any better in those heady times of the early 90s. All they knew was flannel shirts and grunge music.

This movement was coopted by the far-right in the United States – wow, what a surprise. Its precursor was "political correctness," but Cultural Marxism went a step further into xenophobia. We can trace much of the political vitriol of the 2020s to this movement. It was woke before woke was a hated word.

EXTREME MODERNITY

Anytime there is massive political or social upheaval – say from an economic collapse, or a pandemic, or an oaf in the Oval Office, or another economic collapse, or the same oaf back in the Oval Office, there is a rise in conspiracy theories. Of course, all those events were just hypothetical; they couldn't possibly happen in such a short period of time.

As you step into modern times, there are dozens, if not hundreds, of conspiracy theories that have emerged in the last few decades. America has quite the monopoly on modern conspiracies. The book *Conspiracy Nation* explores this phenomenon, but you don't want to read another book. The gist is that after World War II, conspiracy theories rose dramatically in political and cultural life shaping public discourse, policy, and social anxieties. An eroding trust in public institutions combined with a decline in education and an increase in social alienation is the perfect petri dish for new conspiracies and extremist thought to emerge. America is the great melting pot, after all.

The following section gives you a handy overview of the most well-known conspiracies to emerge over the last 80 years in the American zeitgeist.

Government/Alien Cover-Ups

- Roswell 1947 – A "flying disc" rumored to be an alien spacecraft, complete with dead bodies, crashed in New Mexico.

- Men In Black – Government operatives who harass, threaten, or silence people that claim to have seen UFOs. Sometimes they write rap songs too.

- Fake Moon Landing – The U.S. government filmed a fake moon landing instead of actually going there. More on that later.

- Area 51 – Classified military base in Nevada where the government researches crashed UFOs, such as the one from Roswell. Indiana Jones once broke in after finding the Holy Grail.

- Alien Abductions – Hundreds of people have claimed they were taken up into spaceships over the past several decades. We will discuss a specific one in the next chapter.

- <u>Cow Mutilations</u> – Extraterrestrials, secret cults, or the government conducted mysterious dissections of cows, including draining their blood...for some reason.

- <u>Black Helicopters</u> – Unmarked and silent government choppers used by the Deep State to eliminate dissenters or coverup secret operations.

- <u>Chemtrails</u> – The government uses planes to crop dust the population with chemicals. More on this later.

ANTI-COMMUNISM

- <u>John Birch Society</u> – Founded in 1958, a far-right group that promotes the idea of a New World Order that has infiltrated the government, media, and UN to install a socialist global government. What kind of sick freak would want universal, socialist healthcare anyway?

- <u>Red Scare</u> – Big in the 1950s, Senator Joseph McCarthy led investigations based on the idea that the Soviet Union was sending spies to infiltrate the U.S. They got it right with convicted (and executed) spies, the Rosenbergs, but whiffed big with the Hollywood Blacklist.

- <u>Trilateral Commission</u> – Another take on the New World Order / Deep State / elite cabal controlling the world. The commission was a non-governmental organization founded by David Rockefeller to focus on economic policy. However, people believed it was created to merge world economies for a one-world government.

Assassinations

- <u>John F. Kennedy (JFK)</u> – Government did it.

- <u>Martin Luther King, Jr. (MLK)</u> – Government did it.

- <u>Robert F. Kennedy (RFK)</u> – Government did it.

- <u>John Lennon</u> – Government did it. Or possibly Ringo.

- <u>Burger King (BK)</u> – Ronald McDonald is innocent. Government did it.

False Flags

- <u>Sinking of USS Maine</u> – The battleship exploded in 1898 in Cuba, sparking the Spanish-American War. Many believe that Spain deliberately sabotaged it to provoke war with the U.S. It was proven it was caused by an ignition of coal and ammunition.

- <u>Pearl Harbor</u> – There are two similar theories that state the U.S. government knew that Japan was going to bomb the harbor in Hawaii. This was in order to galvanize American public opinion for the war. The Michael Bay film of the same name failed to cover this, an unfortunate oversight.

- <u>Gulf of Tonkin</u> – In August of 1964, U.S. Navy ships were attacked by North Vietnamese forces. This led to the U.S. escalating its involvement in the emerging Vietnam War, which turned out great for all sides. Well, not great. But it did give us a slew of solid movies and rock songs. Many believe the attacks either never happened or were conducted by the U.S.

government to justify entering further into the conflict.

- 9/11 – No, it wasn't Middle Eastern terrorists that took out the Pentagon in Washington, D.C. and the Twin Towers in New York City. It was George W. Bush to help justify the Iraq and Afghanistan wars. This will be discussed in detail later.

- Sandy Hook – The tragic elementary school shooting in 2012 is thought by some to have been planned out by the government with the children and their families serving as hired actors. You will learn more about this later along with its main proponent, Alex Jones.

Like Oreo flavors (what the hell are you smoking over there, Mondelez?), there are a seemingly endless number of conspiracy theories in the United States alone. Like a good conspiracy theorist, you should do your own research if you want to know more. The following sections will dive deeper into the more famous conspiracies. Some of which have already been mentioned.

Heads or Trails

The conspiracy theory of government "chemtrails" is an older one of the modern eras, but it still checks out. The idea behind this one is that governments or secret organizations are secretly using aircraft to add toxic chemicals into the atmosphere. Those "trails" that you see left by airplanes – that is not jet fuel, its chemicals being released. What do the chemicals do? Whatever you want! Sterilization of the population, controlling the weather, mind control that forces the effected people to watch hours of network television every night, lowering life expectancy, chemical warfare, or simply making you dumber than you already are. And you are pretty dumb, especially if you believe in chemtrails. The scientific community has summarily dismissed any of these claims, but why trust them? That is exactly what they want you to believe so you stop asking questions. Be wary of the skies.

Film Me To The Moon

Rising above the lower atmosphere into outer space, we come upon another popular conspiracy theory that has been around for over half a century. This states that the landings on the Moon in 1969 and 1972 were faked.

The premise of this is that we, as humans, have never developed the technology to send astronauts to the moon. Instead, in order to appease the American public during the height of the Cold War, an elaborate sound stage was set up and the "footage" of the landing and walking on the moon was merely props and actors. It was well known that Neil Armstrong was actually played by John Wayne, while Buzz Aldrin's character was portrayed by a rather sloshed Dean Martin.

Figure 2: Behind the Scenes Of The Moon Landing At Studio 6H. Also Where They Filmed Boogie Nights.

The theory trailblazed many others as it utilized bogus science to debunk the fact that we had actually landed on the moon. This is a common tactic in conspiracy theories that will show up throughout this book. Pictures of the landing were criticized because of the way shadows fell in different directions indicating they came from stage lighting rather than the actual Sun. It was also posited that astronauts could not survive Earth's radiation field and that in the pictures, there were no stars visible – except of course for Dean Martin and John Wayne. Finally, the iconic American flag planted in the ground seems to be waving as if it is in the wind, when there is none on the Moon, so how can that be?

Conspirators used science (albeit in a completely wrong way) to boost their credibility of the theory. We can see this today in the more recent theory of "Flat Earth" or in a Roland Emmerich film like *2012* or *The Day After Tomorrow*.

THAT'LL HOLOCAUST YOU

This antisemitic conspiracy theory is a fan favorite, despite being easily discredited by pesky things like videos, photographs, and historical records. As it states, these people believe that the genocide of six million Jews by Nazi Germany during World War II never happened. Oh really? In that case, the Nazis weren't that bad after all. Those six million probably just wandered off. Nothing like a healthy dose of historical revisionism to go with your antisemitism.

This theory originated not long after the last shots of the war. Former collaborators and Nazis attempted to downplay the concentration camps to avoid accountability. By the 1960s, it had gained ground as new followers started to question survivor accounts and the existence of the camps. By the time of the Internet, far-right and Neo-Nazis had this theory well-incorporated into their ideologies, which had plenty of antisemitism mixed in already.

While several European countries have passed laws against Holocaust denial, the theory has spread across the U.S. quickly. The new administration will surely put a stop to it. And if you believe that then you'll likely believe this theory.

ONE PILL, TWO PILL, RED PILL, BLUE PILL

This conspiracy theory emerged in 2012, so it is just a teenager. But it has quickly become an extremist juggernaut in the online world and beyond. The term "red pill" comes from *The Matrix*

(1999), where taking the red pill symbolizes awakening to a hidden truth (the blue pill meant you would stay asleep and never know). In this context, it refers to men believing they have "woken up" to supposed feminist control and male oppression. These men, mostly white and heterosexual are also known as "incels," which is short for "involuntary celibate."

It began on Reddit, the germy doorknob of the Internet, but quickly propagated into a full-blown disease across 4chan, 8chan, Twitter, and YouTube. The major catalyst is known as Gamergate (2014). This was an online harassment campaign by trolls and basement meme lords that targeted women in the video game industry. This toxic masculinity and misogyny in gaming culture metastasized and eventually merged with alt-right movements, particularly QAnon.

You don't have to stop at red though! You could continue onto Black Pill, an extension of the movement that promotes nihilism and hopelessness around gender, dating, and society. It is a fun bunch. So fun in fact, that several domestic terrorists can be traced back to it, including several attacks in Toronto and the United States since 2018.

Raise Your False Flag

If you read the award-winning book, *So You Want To Be A Dictator*, you may already be familiar with the false flag approach. This is where a leader manufactures an attack on the homeland and blames a minority group for carrying it out. This allows the leader to justify taking more power or declaring war on another nation or group.

Some false flag operations may actually be true. They are often grounded enough in reality to merit that. However, conspiracy theorists tend to mark anything and everything as a false flag operation. This is especially true when it fits into their own half-baked narrative of reality. Probably the most famous of these claims is the theory that the George W. Bush administration orchestrated the September 11, 2001, attacks in New York City and Washington, D.C. in order to justify the invasion of

Afghanistan and Iraq. The purpose of the invasion was to topple the reign of Saddam Hussein and claim the vast oil reserves and moustache cream supplies in Iraq.

In order to actually pull off this false flag operation, all George W. Bush had to do was plant bombs within the two World Trade Center towers so they would collapse and melt the steel beams. According to theorists, jet fuel can't melt steel beams as it cannot get hot enough. That's just science. In addition, he had to pay off a few thousand people to keep it quiet, fire a missile at the Pentagon and make people believe it was a plane, cover up any witnesses in two of the most populous cities in America, and convince all of Congress to pass a bill to support the two wars. Super easy, especially for a leader who has the IQ of a collapsed building.

Despite intelligence agencies, the National Institute of Standards and Technology (NIST), most professional architects, scientists, engineers, the 9/11 commission by Congress, and the Department of Defense (DoD) rejecting these claims, the theory continues to hold sway over many people. Can you blame them? Who is going to believe the collective knowledge and science of the government, military, and civilians? (Only sheep and rubes, that is who. And you aren't one of them, are you?)

Figure 3: Someone Who Knows More Than Any Scientist Or Government Organization.

There are dozens – if not hundreds – more theories. These are merely the tip of the iceberg. Speaking of which, did an iceberg really sink the Titanic? Or was it a government hit job to help hide a terrible secret...a secret of...something. Open your eyes, the iceberg is innocent. #GeorgeBushDid1912

In the next chapter, you will learn more about different conspiracy theories, whether baked or – more likely – half-baked. While we have reviewed some theories already, there is a veritable bevy of wild accusations, wacky witch hunts, secretive politics, hidden agendas, baseless speculations, and funny falsehoods galore. You are able to pick and choose which parts of these theories you want and – more importantly – how to use these to persuade others to join your cause and start to fully form your extremism empire.

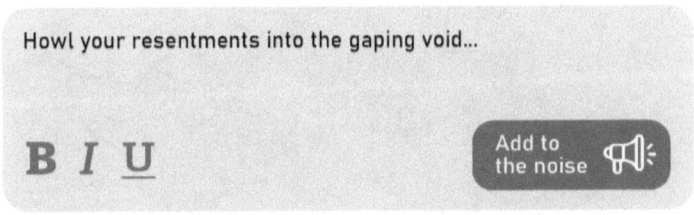

Howl your resentments into the gaping void...

B *I* <u>U</u>

Add to
the noise

Hot-Takes `51,349`   Least hot ↓↑

wafflecopterLOLfactory ✅ 982 days ago

98% of this chapter is 100% wrong. 2% is half-right, but by accident. I've 400 books. To summarise... *(Click to expand...)*

📢 **0**
   Reached

CHAPTER 2

YOU WANT TO BELIEVE

"If you would persuade, you must appeal to interest rather than intellect."

— BENJAMIN FRANKLIN, LADIES' MAN

N ow it is time to learn more about conspiracy theories and begin picking out your favorite ones to latch on to, promote, and utilize. You already learned about several of the more well-known conspiracy theories in the previous chapter, those were only the tip of the iceberg (which, as mentioned earlier, was totally framed by the government).

The reality of these unrealities is that there are so many theories and variations of theories that this book won't possibly be able to capture them all. You may need to "do your own research" to find further nuances that help accommodate your new world view against the New World Order.

These conspiracy theories are divided into three categories based on believability and impact. They follow the parabola of conspiracy theorems (see Figure 4). This parabola provides a basis for measuring the effectiveness of recruiting those to your cause and / or the overall effectiveness of being known and almost credible, which is the most dangerous combination of extremism.

Figure 4: The Parabola of Conspiracies

The first parabolic point is the "Kiddie Pool," which consists of theories based on extremely silly jokes. These are basically benign to the vast majority of the population. They often are associated with a celebrity, accusations of strange behaviors, or weird hobbies.

The vertex of the parabola, also known as the "Wading Pool" conspiracies are based at least somewhat on real science or critical thinking. These theories tend to pull from legitimate sources (or semi-legitimate), and either misconstrue facts, take theories to the wrong conclusion, or completely misunderstand the facts of an event. These are the best for recruiting followers to your cause as they have enough basis in reality to garner interest with a broader populace.

At the far-right side of the parabola is the "Deep End," where we usually see advanced versions of the semi-legitimate based conspiracies from the "Wading Pool." These tend to be incredibly far-right (or left) and dangerous to others, including those who follow the theories. There is only the thinnest connection to reality in these theories, but because they stem from simpler, more rational theories, they have held onto a higher level of believability than they deserve.

Get Your Floaties On

It is time to jump into the Kiddie Pool and get those feet wet with some fun-loving conspiracy theories. These tend to be rather outlandish and silly theories on everything from celebrities to animals to the afterlife. They may not radicalize you or others, but they will tickle your extremism bone.

Caw-Cawspriacy

Birds aren't real. Yep, that is this satirical conspiracy summed up in three words. The premise of this theory, created in 2017, is that birds were replaced by government drones between the 1950s and 1970s meant for tracking us on a day-to-day basis. The "birds" or drones sit on power lines to recharge and defecate on objects or people as a form of tracking device. This is quite literally a conspiracy theory that was created as a joke. Yet, many take it seriously like Dogecoin or American exceptionalism. This makes it at the lowest of the low on the conspiracy parabola, but worth noting because, while this one has remained a joke, some other theories created in the same vein find people taking them far more seriously. Perhaps David Attenborough is covering up a deep, dark secret in his nature documentaries.

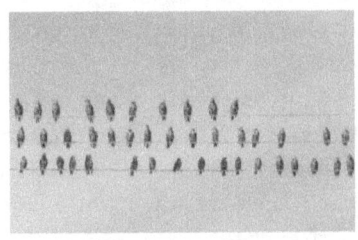

Figure 5: A Whole Flock Of LIES

James and the Giant Afghani

This comical one does in fact have true believers despite its rather flimsy premise. In 2002, U.S. soldiers operating out of garrisons in the Kandahar region of Afghanistan reported seeing giants approach them. It was said they were seen doing normal giant things, cooking food, hunting, skimming through Netflix on What to Watch only to end up watching episodes of *The Office* that they have seen ten times before. It was even said that an entire patrol of U.S. special forces went missing due to the giants. Observers said the beasts stood 13 feet tall, sported flaming red hair, and two rows of teeth for gnashing food. So, it sounds like they just saw Conan O'Brien. The Pentagon has denied all the reports of these giants, but of course that is exactly what they want you to think.

This would be a good one to utilize as it involves fomenting distrust of the government, as they always are hiding secrets from the public. This includes hiding giant former late night hosts.

All Roads Lead To Nowhere

There is an inherent danger in partly understood science. We will see this more in the Wading Area when that danger becomes openly serious with regards to its theories. Grounding the initial idea in science lends it credibility, especially to those who have no science background and thus take everything at face value. In this case, it is a benign misunderstanding of science and history that gives us what is known as Roman Empire Theory.

The theory states that the Roman Empire was never real. You read that correctly. One of the most historically documented civilizations that spanned 1500 years did not exist. So much for Nero, huh? The claim comes from a scrap of papyrus that was discovered (known as the Gallus fragment), found in Egypt. Someone claimed that the writing was Greek and not Latin, since the Roman Empire's language was Latin for documents. This initial idea was taken ever further by stating that everything we claim is from the Romans was from either the Greeks, Phoenicians, or one of the many other civilizations of that time. This means that there was no Caesar, and thus there never would be a Little Caesar's Pizza, and thus there are no $5.00 hot-in-ready deals right now.

The followers of this theory often utilize actual historical facts about the period to back up their claims. This is where partly understood science can be so powerful. You can point to the true parts of your conspiracy theory and use that to justify the bizarre or far-fetched parts. Remember this point because it is a great tool [More on this in Chapter 6] to recruit potential followers. If you do, make sure you protect Little Caesar's hot-in-ready deals. They are only $5.00, now that low price is a conspiracy!

ABDUCTION JUNCTION

He has seen three different types. They are less than four feet tall; they have an "upside-down pear-shaped head." The description goes on and on. They have pointy chins and large black eyes that wrap around the side of their big grey head. This is "The Greys," as told by John Velez. However, it works for a lot of people who claim they were abducted by beings outside of Earth.

This phenomenon of people reporting that they have been kidnapped by extraterrestrials has a long, rich history. There are so many reports, articles, and sightings that they would easily fill up a book on their own or you can simply watch any documentary like *Mars Attacks*, *Independence Day*, or *Alf*. For our purposes and the purposes of brevity, let's look simply into The Greys, which gives a description of the most classic-looking aliens. After all, you surely have heard ad nauseum about Roswell.

Mr. Velez had a close-up of the spacecraft in 1978, seeing a "huge formless football-shaped light." He also saw the classic "saucer-shaped" craft that movies had been using for decades before then, so he clearly didn't get the idea from them. While many abductees claim that they were probed all over their body, John takes it in a bit of a different direction. According to him, the aliens handed him a hybrid alien-human baby who they claimed was John's offspring. He was told – via telepathy from the aliens – that he had six in all, so he could field a basketball team in *Space Jam*. John ended up not taking the babies, which is a shame that they had to grow up with a deadbeat father. They probably ended up getting involved with the wrong aliens, doing drugs, and ending up destitute. Shame on John.

So, why are there so many people like John who believe in alien abductions? A few of the key reasons are that they are suggestible – which is common for most conspiracy theory believers. Other contributors are mental illness and sleep paralysis, which often causes people to see things that aren't there, like six alien children that you abandon and don't pay child support for. Dammit, John, how could you?

Good Vibrations

"Low vibration entities" comes from the spirit world so get out your gemstones for this one. These entities exist in different dimensions and planes of existence to us. This makes it difficult to describe what they look like, how convenient. They represent negative feelings and energy and will feed on them to maintain their presence around humans. They tempt you to do negative things and prevent you from experiencing positive outcomes to events or activities. Basically, they are huge dickheads.

People claim to see them in their dreams or had them in past lives or when you participate in astral travel – which is of course something that people do all the time. Some people claim that certain objects conduct low vibrational energy and thus must be gotten rid of. This includes coffee, alcohol, and most importantly, eyelash extensions – the evilest thing of all, apparently.

This is a great conspiracy theory to potentially latch onto as it can be a cash cow. You can do things like sell "high vibrational objects" or "low vibrational energy deflectors" (just sell some cheap makeup mirrors from China). You'll be making millions and living the high life in Sedona, Arizona in no time.

Dip Those Toes

You may think the shallow end of the adult pool is the safest, but when it comes to conspiracy theories – this is where the true danger lies. Think of it like this, in the shallow end you can wade into the warm waters of conspiracies and fringe, but it is still shallow enough that you can stand on things like science to give your theory legitimacy. Of course, the science you are using will be vastly misconstrued and misused. These theories often have a political or social theme to them, which is why they can often lead to – and have led to – violence. There may be blood in the water, but it is time for you to learn about these conspiracies.

Bot-Eat-Bot World

We will start with something a little less dangerous, but that provides a good example of this Wading Pool effect. The "Dead Internet Theory" states that most of the Internet consists of bots and AI-generated content that prohibits most human activity to manipulate the population. Believers of this theory assert that secretive government agencies created the bots intentionally to push search results and websites they want consumers to receive. These bots were allegedly created in 2016, when the Internet was effectively killed by them. Rest in Peace, the Internet.

In 2016, a security firm released a report that stated over 50 percent of web traffic was made by bots. Thus, this gives believers of this conspiracy a quantifiable leg to stand on to give the Dead Internet Theory credibility. Additionally, the advent of AI models like ChatGPT will be generating most of the Internet's content by 2030. Even *The New Yorker* reported on this phenomenon. Unless AI wrote that article. A kernel of truth can turn into a popcorn of conspiracy.

While perhaps parts of this theory will be true a decade or so down the line, the danger right now is that the claims made from this theory have gained traction. The biggest claim is that the U.S. government, as well as other governments, are the primary actors running these bots and are using them to gaslight the entire world, although if the theory is right, then the government might just be bots gaslighting other bots.

PIZZA PARTY

A man walks into Comet Ping Pong, a pizzeria, in December 2016 and fires three shots from his AR-15 rifle. Edgar Welch later told police after his arrest that he was attempting to save children trafficked by the Deep State from the basement of the restaurant. The one problem was that Comet Ping Pong did not have a basement. This is Pizzagate, and it has been one of the most dangerous conspiracies that morphed out of the larger Deep State umbrella of theories.

Pizzagate emerged during the 2016 election with the accusation that the campaign of Democratic nominee, Hillary Clinton, was involved in a human trafficking and child sex ring. The emails that were stolen off of Clinton's computer were the impetus for this theory, with theorists claiming that they contained coded messages about trafficking. They inferred that when emails contained "CP" it meant "Cheese Pizza" aka "Child Pornography." Yep, that is the hard-hitting investigative journalism that we need as a country.

Figure 6: Corporate Pizza Parties Just Got A Whole Lost More Sinister.

This theory, unsurprisingly, spread like wildfire across the far-right of the United States, even appearing again during the 2020 election. Despite no further findings of any nonexistent basements, the theory has stuck with people and spread beyond the far-right to the fringe on both sides, focusing less on Clinton and more on the worldwide Deep State cabal of the rich and powerful. Besides a fear of topping-less pizza, Pizzagate also gave birth to the QAnon theory, which we will discuss shortly, about the Deep State. Crazy begets crazy. Since the Pizzagate theory has expanded its audience, it is a good place to start your foray into all the Deep State conspiracy goodies, and of course, it will be a goldmine for recruiting others to follow you. Perhaps lay off the pizza aspect though, especially the $5.00 hot-in-ready from Little Caesar's.

RENEW, REUSE, RECYCLE

The Great Replacement Theory is an alt-right conspiracy theory that permeates across the world – at least where there is white people. The theory states that global elites, particularly leftists, have been plotting and orchestrating the replacement of white populations with non-white minorities from other countries. Most of the populist political and social movements around the Western World are built on this theory (whether they admit it or not).

Populism, jingoism, ultra-nationalism, xenophobia, and extremism all borrow from this theory. Two main reasons for this are that it is nearly impossible to prove or disprove (burden of proof) and it taps into people's base fears of being replaced. That is a win-win right there. What makes it so dangerous is how easy it is for scared people to believe; they see new faces in their neighborhood or read about population influxes on the news. It is not a big leap to arrive at the Great Replacement Theory after that. Why look at the true, more complicated reasons of mass migration like war, poverty, and famine? Those things aren't fun.

The theory has been cited by many individuals who are responsible for mass violence, including the Christchurch, New Zealand mosque massacre and the El Paso Walmart shootings of 2019. The theory has only gained more traction as it spreads like wildfire on social media coupled with the continued shift of demographics across the world. Much like the Deep State umbrella, this theory is so ubiquitous across extremists that it would be a crime not to adopt parts of it for your own agenda. Reuse, don't replace.

AVENUE Q

Here you are at the very top of the parabola, smack dab in the middle. QAnon is relatively new on the conspiracy theory scene, but it has rapidly become one of the most influential – and the most dangerous. It has become more than a conspiracy theory and morphed into a political movement as well, culminating in a vast number of believers storming the U.S. Capitol on January 6, 2021. Or perhaps they were just touring it, and it got out of hand, you know how those Federal building tours are – anything goes. The theory states that there is a cabal (they do love cabals, don't they?) of Satanic, cannibalistic child molesters that is operating a global child sex ring and conspired *against* President Trump during the 2020 election. It is never enough that they are rich cannibals, they must bring poor Satan into their theory as well. Hasn't he dealt with enough? Especially with the Satanic panic in the 1980s. Guy needs a break.

Figure 7: Can You Guess The Color Of The Hat?

You will learn about QAnon and their leader, Ron Watkins later. The reason to introduce them here as well is to also learn a bit about the Deep State, their favorite concept. The concept has been around in the United States at least since the 1950s, when an article mentioned a "dual state" of shadowy governments that controls politics. According to *Scientific American*, the prevalence of state secrets has led to a rise in conspiracies about the state. Think of the Central Intelligence Agency (CIA), National Security Agency (NSA), or one of nearly a dozen other agencies that operate in the world of the highly classified. Because they cannot provide a high level of transparency, it raises doubts and questions from your average citizen. Often, learning about previous covert operations, such as what the CIA conducted in the 1960s and 1970s, come to light later and contribute to a growing distrust of the government and thus new theories emerge about a sinister Deep State. Then other "tentacles" of theories pop out from the Deep State, usually with little to no basis, but because the government has hidden activities in the past, people often believe the theories regardless. This is the danger and how offshoot theories like Pizzagate become prevalent. It all stems from the Deep State. Unless you go a fully spiritual route in your extremism, you'll be drinking from the well of the Deep State to build your extremist empire.

Dumbo Days

You are treading water, but this theory still edges itself into the Wading Area category, despite it reaching rather insane conclusions. It is called "Deep Underground Military Bases," and yes, the acronym is appropriately named DUMBs. This is another offshoot tentacle of the overall Deep State, but worth an honorable mention here.

This conspiracy theory states that within these Deep Underground Military Bases, there are children being trafficked by the Deep State and held against their will, sometimes miles underground. Sounds pretty unlikely, right? But wait, there's more. Believers of DUMBs think, that earthquakes are caused by military staff freeing the children from these underground bases and arresting the Deep State members who hid them in these bases. One claim stated that 35,000 malnourished and caged children were rescued by the U.S. military from these bases inside connecting tunnels underneath New York City's Central Park in

2020. The claim on social media eventually had 14,000 shares, although there was never any evidence of its validity.

The poster even claimed they were part of the "Pentagon Pedophile Task Force," which sort of sounds more like the task force is made up of pedophiles than of people searching for them. They may want to rebrand that before they go searching under the sewers of major cities again. As for you, well, don't join that task force, but keep this theory in mind as it does connect well with the larger Deep State theories.

Dive Right In To The Deep End

Don't be scared, the water is deep, but once you dive into the far end of the conspiracy spectrum, you'll find the water more inviting than you think. You'll be swimming in no time, but be careful, the people that believe the theories in this part of the pool may have held their breath too long underneath, causing brain damage. Not you though, you should be fine...probably.

These are the theories that seem as far-fetched as the goofier ones from the Kiddie Pool but are often based on reality to some extent (emphasis on some). Then, they take that reality and murder it in an open field. In short, people take these seriously and perhaps you will, too!

Swiss Miss

In Switzerland, there is a large research facility known as CERN (European Organization for Nuclear Research) – it is a French acronym in case you were wondering why the words don't match up to the letters. It operates the Large Hadron Collider (LHC), which is the world's largest, most powerful particle accelerator. It is meant for exploring and discovering the world of elementary particles and states of matter. Basically, they are doing some really advanced physics trying to find the building blocks of the universe. Unless you have an advanced (or maybe two) degrees in physics, you likely won't understand too much of the intricacies of the work being done at the LHC. That won't stop the conspiracy theorists though!

Figure 8: The LHC, Its Just Science Pipes...Or Is It?

The LHC has a number of different theories based on it. One of the major theories says that scientists are trying to recreate a black hole and if – or when – they do, it will either destroy Earth or open a portal to another dimension that could also destroy Earth. The theme across all of these is that Earth will be destroyed by the Collider in due time. To be fair, the scientists do claim to have tried to create mini black holes to study anti-matter, so you can see how this theory is based to some extent in reality.

Some of the more outlandish claims worth mentioning are that scientists at CERN are using the LHC to open a gateway to Hell and bring out the devil (seriously, give him a break). Or that time travelers have already come through...somewhere, it is unclear where, in the LHC and are in our time period.

As you can see, all of these different theories are based on a grand misunderstanding of the complex science of the LHC. The scientists claim their work is done under strict safety regulations and have no intention of destroying our planet. That is just what they want you to think though, they are clearly part of a Satanic cult of advanced physicists that hold seances and sacrifice children before turning the Collider on. Utilizing this conspiracy theory for your cause means you can claim you are a genius at science and your followers will believe you, especially if you can say something like, "These satanist scientists are trying to find the Higgs Boson, which is part of the Higgs mechanism on elementary particles to open up a portal and kill God." See? You can almost sound smart. Almost.

2D CHESS

You've heard of the Earth in three dimensions, but have you tried looking at Earth in just TWO dimensions? Well, now you can with the Flat Earth conspiracy theory! It has everything you need: bad science, monsters at the end of the ocean, bible misinterpretations, and a special society you can join.

First, let's get something straight. The modern Flat Earth theory is not an official successor or relation to what people in the distant past believed in (and a lot of that is a myth anyhow). With that in mind, let's quickly look back at the OG Flat Earthers.

For millennia, humans believed the Earth was flat or they didn't even think that because they were busy fighting animals to survive. In 600 BCE, after hearing so much bullshit, a scientist named Pythagoras (the eponymous name of that damn mathematical equation) stated that the Earth was, in fact, spherical. Those nerds, Plato and Aristotle also concluded that the Earth was round, and it was after their conclusion that most people came to accept it as fact. It is a myth that people in medieval times thought the Earth was flat and that there were monsters at the end of the oceans. Hell, Christopher Columbus was looking for a western route to India so he could do what he loved most – killing the natives.

In comes Samuel Shenton, who founded the International Flat Earth Society in 1956. In their first meeting, they only served plain, round crackers. Shenton's intent was to reach children and inform them of the government's lies that the Earth was round. He used to say that the myth of the spinning globe was fought against by Einstein, Columbus, and Franklin Delano Roosevelt (FDR) – possibly together as some sort of time traveling, handi-capable, super team. Which, honestly, may be the coolest part of this theory. Maybe they came through the LHC.

Today, the society has around 3,500 card-carrying members. They still probably serve plain, round crackers at their meetings.

As of this year, they believe the Earth is a flat "disc." They had it as a "mixtape" earlier but had to update based on the music industry. They have stuck with disc as "the Earth is shaped like a Spotify playlist" doesn't have the same ring to it.

As funny as this theory is, it still has dangerous tentacles to it. It utilizes pseudoscience – or just patently wrong science – to push its theory and recruit, but this also means that members tend to believe other bad science. The members aren't all uneducated, there are some who are college-educated, and even scientists. It goes to show you that specializing in something doesn't mean you know a lot about any other thing. You could adopt this theory, too; it has the inklings of a Deep State trying to hide the "real Earth" with agencies like NASA. Plus, you may get some scientists to join your cause. Just don't try to replicate the pseudoscience referenced to prove the planet is flat. One guy did that, and well...he joined another flat society.

COLD-BLOODED

They live among us. They inhabit our celebrities, politicians, and even everyday people. They are the Lizard People, the reptilian humanoids. They are us. No, that isn't the start of the next Jordan Peele flick. Although, Jordan, think about it, the author has a script treatment and everything.

This is the Lizard People theory, first popularized by radio show host David Icke in 1999. Icke said shapeshifting lizard-like aliens controlled everything on Earth and that many world leaders were actually these creatures in disguise.

However, it has been around longer than that. It started in the 1940s, when an American occultist, Maurice Doreal, described a serpent race that lives among us. People have since picked up on this theory and it has even popped up in politics across the United States and Canada.

This theory is at least based in some truth because as we know from the previous book and Man Booker Prize Winner, *So You Want To Be An Oligarch*, Mark Zuckerberg is likely a lizard person. However, outside of that, there is no confirmation that anyone else is a shapeshifting alien. If you decide to adopt this theory, you'll likely have a few Congresspeople on your side, but you may need to combine it with the next theory to truly bonify your conspiracy credentials.

LASER HAIR REMOVAL

A U.S. Congressperson came up with this doozy of a deep-end theory. We won't spend too much time on it, but it shows a tentacle theory and how bizarre you can truly take things, even when you are in power.

Figure 9: A Jewish Space Laser As Seen From The
International Space Station

Marjorie Taylor Greene. She is a United States representative from Georgia. In 2018, during the California Wildfires, Representative Greene stated that the fires were created by "Jewish space lasers." The quotes are there to indicate that none of this shit is made up. She said these lasers or "solar space generators" were powered by the Rothschild Family (a Deep State favorite) as well as a conglomeration of shadowy government individuals. Either way, this is a great theory to adopt as you already will have some pull in government and anything that is anti-Jew, like this theory, is also anti-Deep State. You can get people to throw themselves on to the idea that Jewish people have lasers in fucking space while still governing a country. What a deal.

MASK-QUERADE

If you remember the year 2020, which at this point was sometime around 400 years ago with how it feels, you'll remember that nothing significant ever happened. The end.

Oh wait, there was a worldwide pandemic – or if you will – not a "pandemic." For the true believers, COVID-19 was nothing more than a government conspiracy orchestrated by the evil Dr. Anthony Fauci, who was the Director of the National Institute of Allergy and Infectious Diseases and Advisor to the President during the so-called pandemic. He also had help from the Chinese and Bill Gates.

The reigning theory of truth is that sometime in late 2019, the COVID-19 virus was created in a lab in Wuhan, China and then spread by 5G cell phone towers across the globe. See how aspects of this are true? That is how you entrap people.

5G has been a favorite topic for conspiracy theorists even before the pandemic. It has often been attributed to the spread of cancer through its radiofrequencies and that it spreads low levels of radiation to lower your immune system.

As the "so-called virus" spread into cities everywhere, mask mandates came into effect as well as other bans on travel and public gatherings. At the same time, the idea emerged that the virus was fake and was simply a way for the government to control its people by forcing them to stay inside and wear cloth masks. The idea of the COVID-19 and 5G being linked spread nearly as fast as the virus itself, popping up all over social media, in particular, that bastion of truth, Tik Tok.

Once the vaccine was made available, believers rejected it. They claimed the government was using the syringes to inject people with 5G microchips, which could be used to control their minds using 5G frequency waves. Governments can then force their citizens to believe what they told them to believe, like that you need to upgrade your cell phone every year. Although plenty of people don't need a microchip to believe that malarkey. Conspiracy theorists were so convinced by the link between 5G and Coronavirus, that 5G towers around the world were burned down by believers. Take that T-Mobile!

There are plenty more conspiracies that fit up and down the parabola, which will be discussed in later chapters as you continue your journey to a full-fledged extremist. Now that you have a good grip on several – and a looser grip on reality – it is time to test yourself. Before you can learn more about how to become an extremist, you will be tested to help you understand and realize your true extremist potential. It is time to tap into your gut feeling while you starve what is left of your brain.

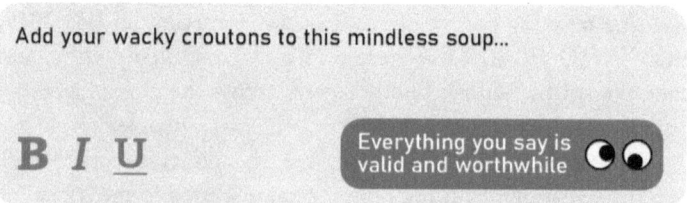

Add your wacky croutons to this mindless soup...

B *I* <u>U</u>

Everything you say is valid and worthwhile

Soup-Words 4

Loosest Connection ⬇⬆

PeterNavarro_author_2   ✔ 59 seconds ago

IF we keep letting kids learn about feelings in school, next they'll be marrying toasters and outlawing ladders. I mean, have you ever eaten a fake burger? Oh yeah "sure" it tastes like meat, WHILE the Chinese are busy installing 6G in every livingm all over the world. Wake the **** up, people, we are THIS close to the abyss.

👀 71

Dur Durr Duuuurrrrrs

CHAPTER 3

REALITY IS WHAT YOU MAKE
OF IT

"Misconceptions play a prominent role in my view of the world."

— GEORGE SOROS, SUPREME OVERLORD OF
THE DEEP STATE BLOOD CABAL

Y ou now have an arsenal of conspiracy theories at your disposal. You also understand the intricacies of these theories and, most importantly, what comprises an extremist. It is time to venture further into the wild recesses of this world. Extremism has a multitude of actors that helped perpetuate the theories that come with it. In the past several decades, many of these actors have become popular through social media and through the bizarreness of recent events.

STICKS AND JONES MAY BREAK BONES

Alex Jones, one of the most popular extremists of our time, deserves first billing here. This unpopped, festering boil of a human being has been at the forefront of conspiracies and extremism for several decades. His empire, Infowars, at its height boasted a popular podcast, television show, website, line of women's lingerie, vitamins, a low-calorie sparkling water, and a syndicated radio show. He is truly a renaissance extremist.

Jones started frolicking down the crazy lane after the events at Waco, Texas in 1993. This was the deadly conflict between whether or not Texas BBQ was better than Kansas City BBQ. Many lives were lost. Perhaps it was when the U.S. federal government conducted a siege on the compound of a cult known as the Branch Davidians, ending in the death of 76 people. Jones claimed a group of unseen forces were controlling the levers of power and keeping things hidden from us, like the secret of the best BBQ sauce.

Jones will pop up throughout this book, but a few things to note regarding his extremist views:

- Stated that the mass shooting murders at the elementary school, Sandy Hook, was a "false flag" operation perpetrated by anti-gun activists and that the parents of the slain children were "crisis actors" hired by this operation.

- Stated that the owner of Comet Ping Pong pizzeria in Washington, D.C. had a basement that was used by Democrats and Hillary Clinton to abuse children and sacrifice them to their demonic god.

- Stated that the white male who ran over protesters at the 2017 "Unite the Right" rally was a "crisis actor" and part of a false flag operation to turn support against god-emperor Donald Trump.

- Stated that the government was adding hormones into the water supply that was turning the frogs gay and thus would turn the rest of the population into BBQ-hating gay frog people. The science is still out on this claim.

Alex has so much knowledge about the underworld of conspiracies that his face is bulging with it. You will continue to read about him as we venture further into the deepest annals of extremism.

Jenny, I Got Your Number

Who better to give deep, scientific, and medical advice than a *Playboy* model and B-level actress? And while Dr. Anthony Fauci looks amazing in the March 1994 issue, for your purposes we will be looking at the October 1993 Playmate of the Month, Jenny McCarthy.

Autism is a neurodevelopmental disorder that affects a small portion of the population. Those diagnosed with Autism tend to struggle with social cues, social situations, and society in general. Ms. McCarthy, in 2007, declared that her son, who she had with Jim Carrey, was autistic due to shots he received as a baby. The baby began to only quote *The Mask,* and it was, frankly, quite disturbing. Although, not quite as disturbing as *The Son of the Mask.*

This brilliant line of reasoning from Ms. McCarthy was the shot heard round the world, leading to the beginnings of what is now known as the "Anti-vax Movement." Thankfully, there wasn't any global pandemic that would require mass inoculations.

Beyond just a global pandemic, the rates of once-nearly-eradicated diseases have popped back up in the U.S. in recent years, such as measles, mumps, and whooping cough. The science remains firm that Autism and similar maladies are not caused by vaccinations, but perhaps by shitty movie sequels or watching Ms. McCarthy on *The View.*

Not Your Average Joe

The once-proud host of the Emmy-losing show, *Fear Factor,* has gone on to be an even prouder host of his own podcast with followers in the millions. A majority of them are on the younger side. This level of fame has gone to his head, no doubt, and is only a small step up from making people eat live cockroaches on television.

Joe Rogan has broadcast some of the worst, most damaging conspiracy theories on his podcast. He does it in a most annoying fashion, by "asking questions" and trying to see things from both sides. This is a talent you will learn later in this book. The act of trying to look at both sides is bullshit – a wonderful level of bullshit that you will learn how to produce yourself.

"The only time I commit to conspiracy theories is when something way retarded happens. Like Lee Harvey Oswald acting alone." Yep, that is a real quote from Joe Rogan. Possibly, his most well-known ability is to bring on quack doctors or other "scientists" who then share their insane beliefs. This allows them to be legitimized, and Joe often gives them softball questions to help promote their platform further.

AGENT ORANGE

Diaper Don was obviously going to make an appearance here. He has the biggest microphone in the country – if not the world – in which he spews hate-filled rhetoric and conspiracy theories that he read while sitting on the toilet.

Speaking of toilets, Trump, during his first presidency, touted the use of swallowing bleach, taking horse worm medication, and blasting UV light directly up your ass to combat COVID-19. He did this on a podium with the symbol of the White House behind him. Thus, America reached its peak absurdism and has never recovered.

Trump also championed one of the classic conspiracies that Barack Obama was born in Kenya. Obama eventually caved and provided to the media his long form birth certificate, which proved...he was born in the goddamn United States. This is another method you will learn in this book that often, even the stupidest, most asinine conspiracies, when forced on others, forces them to try to disprove it – and thus legitimizes it. We will discuss this "firehose" of bullshit later in the book. Trump already has fire hosed plenty of bullshit in the media and in his pants.

Q-tee Pie

Among the names listed so far, this is likely one you may not be as familiar with as compared to the others. But, Ron Watkins has touched your life (without permission) more than you know. He is the creator – and de facto leader – of QAnon.

"CodeMonkeyZ" as he goes by online, was the former operator of 8chan. Let's take a step back and look at the online communities of hate and craziness to put this all into perspective. See Figure 10 to help you understand further.

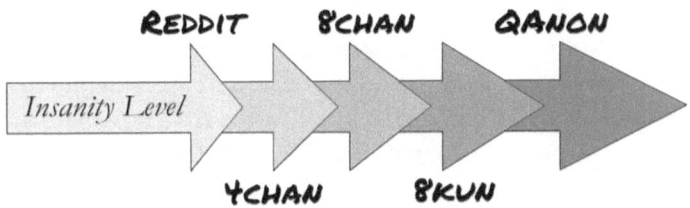

Figure 10: The Progression Diagram of Internet Insanity

Reddit is one of the top five most popular websites in the world with millions of users across thousands of channels where memes, graphics, videos, and chats are shared. At some point, certain sub-groups became too intense and, sometimes, illegal to operate. They were kicked out and moved to 4chan, which had less oversight and far more weirdos. However, that wasn't enough for the Watkins group, and they moved further into Crazy Town (the place not the band) and formed 8chan.

8chan (or 8kun) is where QAnon was born and raised – a rotten hive of pedophilia, misogyny, pro-rape, anti-government, anti-Islam, pro-Rogan, pro-Nazism, pro-life, and pro-Calliou. OK, that last one is made up, but Calliou deserves to be part of this group of deplorables and deserves to die. Fuck that kid.

QAnon comes from the theory that a person named "Q," who had special Q Clearance (it's real, but usually for those who work on nuclear powerplants), had been sharing exclusive high-level government secrets to the 8chan community. This community was instrumental in gathering the totally-not-insane right wing conservatists that tried to overthrow the U.S. government on January 6th, 2021. All of this coming from a guy living in the Philippines. Watkins has since moved to an even poorer, deprived area – Arizona.

Figure 11: For All Your Most Depraved Needs And Yoga Tips

TEST YOUR MANIA

Before we explore the nature of reality and the methods of how to harness it to your will, let's take a quick quiz to ensure you lack the intelligence, critical thinking, and at the same time, have the courage to promote your beliefs about the true nature of the world.

1. You are a normal, law-abiding citizen who lives in a middling urban center. Yesterday, while you were shopping for a new flannel jacket and Kevlar vest, a domestic terrorist went into the strip mall and shot many people using their AR-15 (that they have every right to own). Do you:

A.) Provide the local police and FBI with a detailed account of the incident.

B.) Immediately find the local news station and give them your account of the event.

C.) Say nothing to the government because who knows what they may want from you.

D.) Talk to the media about how this shooting is a false flag operation propagated by a consortium of Deep State anti-flannel mercenaries.

2. You are the host of a mildly popular podcast that caters mostly to white male listeners. Recently, the government has begun to discuss vaccine mandates to stem the tide of a new avian flu emerging rapidly across the country. Do you:

A.) Allow several government officials and scientists on to your podcast to present their facts about the health crisis and the importance of inoculations to provide a fair and balanced view on the situation.

B.) Allow several government officials and/or scientists to provide their viewpoint on your podcast, but you treat them harshly because their views go against your corporate sponsors.

C.) State on your podcast that the scientists are paid for by George Soros and the sick patients on the mainstream news are merely "Crisis Actors."

D.) Go on a rambling tirade about the end of civilization because of these potential mandates and discuss how your patented "Man Cream" is the only way to fight back against avian flu.

3. You are the head of a nationally syndicated newspaper. It is your responsibility to report the news, but, more importantly, to make a profit for the newspaper's owner. This month, the national capital was stormed by thousands of angry citizens attempting to shut down the government. Do you:

A.) Ask all of your reporters to present an in-depth report on the event and what was the catalyst for it to inform readers.

B.) Ensure an article is written, but shove it down to after the Sports page, because there is some hot gossip about Timothée Chalamet that is far more important to your readers.

C.) Talk about how this is a "both sides" issue and play down the actions of the rioters because they still buy your paper, even if they cannot read it properly.

D.) Do absolutely fuck all.

4. You are the chief of a local police force based out of a southwestern U.S. state. This morning, a terrible accident occurred when a commercial passenger plane collided with a military vehicle, resulting in over two dozen casualties. Do you:

A.) Take responsibility regarding the event, work with the military and civilian representatives for rescue efforts and to better understand the situation.

B.) Blame the horrible event on DEI hires in the military who were somehow responsible for the mix-up that led to the collision.

C.) Blame it on the Deep State, indicating the plane was carrying Deep State actors who were on their way to the capital to color tray tables socialist red.

D.) Do absolutely fuck all.

5. You are a prominent government official who is up for reelection this year. Your opponent from the other party seemingly (in public records at least) has no issues regarding their background. Do you:

A.) Conduct a fair and ethical campaign that highlights the important actions and policies you have taken and passed for your district.

B.) Utilize facts to disparage your opponent, who has hidden certain aspects of their life that could ruin their campaign.

C.) Accuse your opponent of drinking the blood of Catholic babies.

D.) Both B and C, with an emphasis on C.

6. You are a second-year college student born into a wealthy family. Recently, several hundred students at your univer-

sity have begun to stage nonviolent protests based on a war in the Middle East that you happen to be on the other side of. Do you:

A.) Allow your fellow students to continue to exercise their right to lawful assembly and protest.

B.) Conduct a similar nonviolent protest to exercise your rights and bring a balanced opinion on the war to others at your university.

C.) Insist – through gathering a crowd of your white, fraternity brothers– that the protests are paid for by the liberal, antifa, uber-woke left. You then bully, intimidate, and make racist remarks to the protesting students via social media and online direct messaging.

D.) Do option C and also avoid any punishment because your parents paid for the university football team's locker rooms.

7. You are a working-class voter who has been struggling for years just to make ends meet. You have seen the rich get wealthier, while you and your family are barely eking out a living as the prices of groceries climbs ever higher despite your paycheck remaining the same. A major election is coming up. Do you:

A.) Consider the choices for leaders carefully, weighing especially the economic policies of the candidates that may provide relief for your family and vote based on those principles.

B.) Don't vote.

C.) Vote for the third party like an idiot.

D.) Realize that the reason egg prices are so high is because a massive invasion of radioactive migrants stole all the chickens for blood sacrifices. Thus, vote for the candidate who gives false promises to save all the chickens and lower prices while doing the funky chicken dance on the campaign.

Congratulations! If you answered either C or D throughout the previous quiz, then you have all the fire and brimstone deep inside of you to become a true extremist. In the next chapter, we will work toward honing your raw determination, hallucination, and irrationalization as you move toward the far end of the spectrum.

Add some alternative facts to the conversation...

B *I* <u>U</u>

See what happens 📢

Comments 98,094   Популярный ⬇⬆

 TheNewPerspectiveRU ✔ 982 days ago

Very interesting point, fellow American citizen. But have you considered that your elections are rigged, your vegetables contain oestrogen (makes gay), and Putin make better leaders than democracy? Just saying. #TruthFromVolgograd

📢 156k
Reached

CHAPTER 4

QUESTION EVERYTHING, BELIEVE NOTHING

"I don't like them putting chemicals in the water that turn the friggin' frogs gay."

— ALEX JONES, SENTIENT HEMORRHOID

The great extremists of the world didn't just spontaneously emerge from nothing. They each followed their own path – whether it be socio or psycho – to the upper echelons of the Illuminati pyramid of extremism. This chapter will teach you how to move from your humble, sane beginnings to become the tinfoil hat of justice against the elites of the underground world that others are too naïve to find for themselves.

There are many different types of extremists you can emulate. You have your choice of all the colors of the extremist rainbow. Mostly.

Remember, you do not have to necessarily believe in any conspiracy theory, that is up to you and how you interpret reality. The key here is that by the end of this book, you will be able to exploit other like-minded (or not so like-minded) people to your extremist cause(s). This will be the best way for you to control them so they can buy whatever bullshit products you will sell [More on this in Chapter 8]. For now, read on and learn. Then decide what is true and what isn't. Embrace the extremism ahead.

PERFECTLY IRRATIONAL

The core catalyst to start your extremist journey is to remove any semblance of critical thinking you may have. Thankfully, if you are already this far in the guide, you likely didn't have much rational thought to begin with, which is a great thing! So pat yourself on your irrational back.

A 2021 study by *Applied Cognitive Psychology* associated low critical thinking ability with a higher belief in conspiracy theories. You may already consider yourself a "free thinker." Most extremists do. You should state this to everyone you know and also just to random strangers on the street. The more you yell it, the more it becomes true. Several other phrases you should learn to yell include:

- "Open your eyes, Sheeple!"
- "Get your heads out of the sand and look up!"
- "Don't be a thought slave, free your mind!"
- "Don't listen to the lamestream media, do your own research!"
- "Think for yourself before they do the thinking for you!"
- "This isn't freedom! This is 1984!"
- "Big [Pharma, Government, Retail] is lying to you!"
- "Disney's live action movies are brilliant, and they should keep making them!"

With any of these statements, people will know you have lost all critical thinking skills. You are well on your way to becoming a free thinker, unchained from the prisons of rationality or society.

Let's be clear, getting rid of critical thinking does not mean you are stupid. No, on the contrary, you have a higher intelligence than those compliant rubes you are shouting at. In fact, a 2023

National Institutes of Health (NIH) study claimed that critical thinking (or lack thereof) is not directly related to intelligence. To quote, "Critical thinking can more completely account for many everyday outcomes, such as how thinkers reject false conspiracy theories, paranormal and pseudoscientific claims, psychological misconceptions, and other unsubstantiated claims. Deficiencies in the components of critical thinking (in specific reasoning skills, dispositions, and relevant knowledge) contribute to unsubstantiated belief endorsement in ways that go beyond what standardized intelligence tests test." Get all that?

This explains why people who are extremely smart in one or two areas, such as surgeons or CEOs, often lack important critical thinking skills and thus believe in conspiracies. Another example of this phenomenon is what is known as "Nobel Disease." There have been several cases (enough for it to be named) of former Nobel Peace Prize winners embracing scientifically unsound or just flat out insane ideas later in their life. The honor of winning the ultimate professional achievement in your field creates a belief in winners that their ideas and judgements should never be questioned again. For example, physicist Brian Josephson won at the age of 22 but spent the remainder of his life chasing odd ideas like telepathy and psychokinesis. The co-founder of DNA, Linus Pauling, thought that Vitamin C could cure cancer. No need to bother with that fancy chemotherapy, just pop some Emergen-C and that leukemia will clear right up, Little Billy.

Figure 12: When Life Gives You Cancer, Make Lemonade.

Free Agency

According to studies, conspiracy theories do not help lessen anxiety even though that is why people tend to believe and propagate them. But why believe those closed-brain scientists? They haven't seen the truth like you. However, it is good to know what the other side says, that way you know your enemy and how to combat their lies. These liars say that rather than conspiracy theories suppressing anxiety, they actually suppress a person's autonomy and sense of control, making them less inclined to take actions that would give them back their agency. Conspiracy theories provide a person with a greater expressive outlet (e.g., yelling at people on the street or online). Again, don't worry, the conspiracy theories that you embrace will help you take agency away from your future followers. It will ensure you hold on to your extremism kingdom that you are building.

Questions and Non-Answers

Another important trait you need to develop early in your journey is that of the needlessly inquisitive. This has two meanings. One, you must learn how to continuously ask questions in bad faith. That means asking questions that experts or those who have differing beliefs cannot possibly answer because there is no answer. Two, it cuts the same way when others ask you questions, you can avoid ever providing any meaningful answer and then accuse the other side of the same thing you do when asking questions. Projection is the name of the game. Let's look at a few ways you can exploit this relationship between questions and non-answers.

- *Question:* How can the Earth be round when we have no way of seeing it?

- *Question:* How can Hillary Clinton not be a pedophile when we haven't seen all her emails about pedophilia?

- *Question: How can 9/11 not be an inside job when George W. Bush may or may not have played Microsoft Flight Simulator?*

See how that works? You put the scenario you want to be true within the actual question and force the person you asked to prove a negative. It is nearly impossible to do this so you will win the argument. It is a perfect tool for the aspiring extremist. The same goes for non-answers.

- *Answer: I did my research at www.flatearthisreal.-geocities.com.*

- *Answer: I spoke to someone who has inside knowledge of George Soros's death cult, but I cannot reveal their name. It is real though.*

- *Answer: The moon landings just do not make sense, the science doesn't back it up, and I would know as I fell asleep to plenty of episodes of Bill Nye.*

Once again, you can cut through any logic in questions and force the asker to validate rather than you having to do the work to prove your point. Always put the burden of proof and the work associated with it on the other party when having a debate.

REALITY BITES

What is reality? This is something you must learn to question constantly. According to the dictionary, reality is parcels of land and structures owned by an individual. Wait, no, that is *realty*. Or is it?

Simply put, reality is an aggregate explanation for what exists in our known universe. Yet, scientists and priests still grapple with the true nature of reality and to understand everything that there is in our world and beyond. The closer they seem to get with new discoveries, the further the nature of reality seems. That is because they are looking in the wrong places such as in astronomy, mathematics, philosophy, and the 1980s film, *The Gods Must Be Crazy*.

As a fledgling extremist reading this guide, you are getting the inside track on learning about the entirety of reality. The only "reality" for you is reality television, which is totally not scripted.

The scientist Carl Sagan once said: "For me, it is far better to grasp the Universe as it really is than to persist in delusion, however satisfying and reassuring." However, he is dead, so how smart could he have really been? You're alive and with a hefty dose of delusion, you can change reality to ensure you never die.

A GRAND DELUSION OF GRANDEUR

Delusion is one of the greatest mental tools you have to dispose of any facts, reason, or science that aims to explain reality.

Studies estimate that anywhere between 15 and 100 out of 100,000 people develop psychosis each year, which includes delusions and hallucinations. This usually occurs with people in their late teens to mid-20s. But why limit yourself to some scientific study? It is probably government controlled. You can develop those delusions at any time in your life if you truly believe in yourself and if you truly believe in the fact that voices are criticizing you through your old RCA television. There are a few time-tested ways to cultivate your delusional thoughts and fantasies.

- <u>Withdraw Socially</u> – Start to remove yourself from your close friends and family, especially if they are rational-thinking humans. Only you know the truths that they will no longer be willing to hear, so spend a lot more time alone and online. There are plenty of echo chambers to help validate your newfound delusions [More on this in Chapter 5].

- <u>Stop Sleeping</u> – Sleep is exactly when the government goons and Lizard People can get you. Freddy

Krueger? Yeah, he is a government stooge. That's what the *Nightmare on Elm Street* movies were trying to warn you about. The less sleep you get, the more you will start to see visions that go beyond the base reality, which the secret elites of the world broadcast to keep you docile.

Figure 13: The government never sleeps, neither should you.

- <u>Get Intense</u> – It ain't called "extremist" if you are going to be demure and mindful. It is time to work on that voice in pitch, frequency, and level of slurring. You need to embrace the strange feelings bubbling inside of you, the tingles emanating from your chest to your limbs. There is a fire inside of you that needs to be released and built upon the oxygen-rich environment that is a right-wing protest – or like a Chuck-E-Cheese birthday party. Let out your carbon dioxide-dense proclamations of the "real" real world.

- <u>Suspect Everything</u> – Stop trusting everyone and everything, no matter how legitimate they or it seem. It is false. You need to increase your level of paranoia to dictator-like levels (refer to Purple Heart Awardee, *So You Want To Be A Dictator* for additional information on paranoia). This level of paranoia will help metastasize your delusions and the theories that come with it. You must suspect everyone, even this author. Don't worry, the author has already suspected you and that cancels this all out, so you are safe. Let's move on. Shift those eyes in love, not hate.

Once you have successfully learned each of these tactics and are exercising them in your delusion of – hopefully – grandeur, then you are ready to move on to choosing your extremist "suit of armor." The next chapter will help you customize your baseline extremism into the tinfoil tinpot titan that you are ready to become.

ReTruths 51,349   Truest ⬇⬆

TheFinalWord ✔ 982 days ago

Actually, the sun IS closer than the moon because IT LOOKS bigger. It's called 'perspectology' - google it. How else could we FEEL warm, right? It's OBVIOUS til you Think about it.

📢 87
Re-Truths

CHAPTER 5

CRAFTING YOUR CRAZY

"You know, a long time ago being crazy meant something. Nowadays, everybody's crazy."

— CHARLES MANSON, WELL-ADJUSTED
INDIVIDUAL

Now that you have reached deep inside to reformat your vision of reality, it is time to look outward. After all, extremists cannot push their message if they are dressed in rags. This is not just about QAnon-wear though, it is about further crafting your image and finding a nuanced version of your extremism. Let us first look at the types of extremists you can be – all including a fun activity for you to choose your favorite type of extremism as well as another to format your beliefs in the most extremist way possible.

Think of this activity like MadLibs, where you pick random nouns and verbs to fill in blanks and create full sentences. In this case, that full sentence will become your very own conspiracy theory.

Regular Noun	Phrase	Extremist Noun	Final Sentence
Government	Is run by	Lizard people	The government is run by the lizard people who are spiking our drinking water to turn us liberal.
Atmosphere	Is made up of	Anthrax-laden nanobots	The atmosphere is made up of anthrax- laden nanobots who are slowly poisoning us with high fructose corn syrup.
The President / Prime Minister	Is really part of the	International Group of Pizza-Loving Pedophiliacs	The President is really a part of the international group of pizza-loving pedophiliacs who are stealing our children and our small change.
Earth's Crust	Is actually composed of	The reincarnated body of Tupac Shakur	Earth's crust is actually composed of the reincarnated body of Tupac Shakur who was never killed but died saving us from a volcanic eruption Sean Combs's baby oil.
The Universe	Is ruled by	Jewish Artificial Intelligence	The Universe is ruled by Jewish AI that has controlled everything for profit since the Big Bang, which was their first move to create human life, which they have been trying to destroy since.

These are just examples, but feel free to switch up nouns and verbs to make your own unique conspiracy theory that your remnant of a mind can think of in its few moments of senility each day. Let's move on to learning about and choosing what label you want as an extremist. Especially now that you have an initial conspiracy theory to lean on as a foundation.

Religious Extremist

The most quoted term by Karl Marx – other than "surf party USA" – is "religion is the opium of the people." That is exactly what this label of extremist encapsulates. It is like a combined shot of heroin with cocaine, which is known as a speedball. You'll feel like Anthony Kedis, lead singer of the Red Hot Chili Peppers. Except, you won't make as good of music as he did. You'll just be really, really high. It could be worse.

According to the Pew Research Center, there are as many as 6 – 7 billion people (85 percent of the total world population) that practice some sort of religion. With that many people, there are bound to be a few freethinkers.

Becoming a religious extremist (or fanaticist) is by far the easiest extremist label to adopt. They have a well-established system that you can tap into immediately.

There are so many different religions to choose from as well and the author will likely anger most of them by the end of this book. There are Catholics, Christians, Muslims, Jews, Protestants, Buddhists, Jainists, Sikhs, and Shintos. Oh my. Even one of the members of Jedisim killed a bunch of kids. Not just the kids, the women, too. He killed them all. They were like animals. He slaughtered them like animals. Darth Vader was not the best prophet, but at least he *only* killed the children. That is more than what can be said about what Catholic priests have been accused of in the past couple of decades.

Perhaps you do not want to go that far. Murder isn't always the best way to get others on your cause and to keep the cause going (except if you are murdering a U.S. healthcare CEO). Start your religious extremism with something closer to supporting laws against abortion or by starting a new Crusades or by screening a Kirk Cameron movie. The world is your holy oyster when it comes to religious extremism. It may not produce pearls, but it'll get the job done.

RIGHT-WING EXTREMIST

THIS SECTION IS IN ALL CAPS BECAUSE THAT IS HOW A RIGHT-WING EXTREMIST – ERR, A TOTALLY STABLE AMERICAN INDIVIDUAL – SPEAKS. We will go ahead and not do that for the rest of this section, but it is important to note at the beginning how you should be talking and promoting your right-wing extremism.

While there are a multitude of factors that contribute to the system of right-wing extremism – they all stand on two core beliefs. The first is a deep distrust of the government. This is that pesky Deep State. They believe the federal government is corrupt and illegitimate, whose leaders are trying to disarm citizens (e.g., "get yer dem hands off my 2nd amendment") and enforce totalitarian – and socialist – control. The Sovereign Citizen movement is a popular offshoot that argues no government has any authority of a person. They even have their own license plates, how cute. Secondly, right-wingers believe in a New World Order (NWO) that is comprised of the United Nations, World Economic Forum, and rich elites who meet in Davos, Switzerland to establish a single world government. Unlike the Deep State that operates more in the shadows, the NWO is in the open as it is tied to more established international authorities. However, right-wingers tend to interchange the two when expressing their thoughts IN ALL CAPS.

Some of the most well-known groups that operate under the right-wing umbrella include the Proud Boys, Aryan Nations, Patriot Front, and Neo-Nazis. Can you guess what else they have in common? A gold star for you if you can figure it out.

Hating a certain set of people isn't all they do though. Right-wingers are gung-ho and gun-ho about their right to bear arms. This is why they are one of the most dangerous extremist groups. Their guns are their last line of defense against a tyrannical government. Groups like the Oath Keepers and the Three Percenters are active, armed militias who have been involved in violent resistance and marches in the US and Canada.

Figure 14: This truck actually needs more flags, pathetic.

American right-wing-ism is a rather new form of extremism, which has been augmented by the ubiquitousness of social media. You do not necessarily need to be adept at technology. You do need to be adept at hanging flags off the back of your lifted truck that you overpaid for and will be in debt because of for the next sixty years. Don't forget to buy that extended warranty. That'll show how crazy you really are. You needn't worry, your life expectancy is worth far less than your high-interest loan. You'll be able to leave the rest of it to the family that you alienated.

Right wing extremism isn't just an American phenomenon, it is just – like most things American – the loudest. Europe has a healthy right-wing extremist environment across most of its countries, too. As of June 2024, several of the most right-wing fringe political movements gained seats in the European Parliament. They came from France, Italy, Germany, the Netherlands, and several other European countries. You will learn more about several of these groups later in the book. Right-wing is almost mainstream in Europe as of this writing. America, are you really going to let the Europeans beat you out in this area? The results of the 2024 elections was a resounding, "No."

Woke Me Up Before You Go Go

You have a singular mission. You are to hate all that is "woke." What is woke? Well, what isn't woke? These rhetorical questions are just the beginning of a litany of inane inquisitions you will be asking the general public throughout your life as an extremist.

Let's talk a bit about "wokeness," as that is what is most important to you as a right-wing extremist.

Like most concepts, "woke" was coopted by right-wing extremists, who took it from the Black community. It began around 2010 in universities and originally meant that someone was (or should be) alert to racial prejudice and discrimination. This definition broadened to include awareness of pertinent issues about the LGBTQ+ community, sexism, and the entire rich tapestry of other social inequalities.

This movement of political correctness across U.S. college campuses – and presumably campuses around the world that don't charge much for admission – led to a backlash from the far-right. The far-right chose to take "woke" for their own purposes, rather than coming up with their own term to express their outrage. Woke has become the favorite rallying cry for the far-right and it can be yours too, although extremist terminology evolves quickly. The newest term they skewer (as of 2024) is DEI or "Diversity, Equity, and Inclusion." It is used as a derogatory term for anything that even resembles offending the beliefs of the far-right, which are fairly thin to start. Regardless, feel free to interchange "DEI" and "woke" when broadcasting conspiracies and the evil doers who are conspiring against you and your kind in the far-right. It is not like you are a Nazi or anything. Right....Right? Far-right.

Left-Wing Extremist

Why yes, the left also is a nice area for you to explore your extremism potential. Left-wing extremism is a collective term that describes any group or person that treats freedom and social equality as absolutes. This is most often paired with anarchist and communist ideals, although those may not always drive the left-winger.

The main ire of the left-wingers is capitalism, which they consider the root of all evil. The hilarious hypocrisy of this belief is that left-wingers are often rich, white kids from affluent families that like to cosplay as revolutionaries because they hate their banker dad. Mostly because he always wants to watch *Wall Street* while they want to watch *V for Vendetta*.

If you tried and failed to be an oligarch (see Grammy Award Winner For Best Spoken Album, *So You Want To Be An Oligarch* to learn more), then this may be a good route for you to pursue. Instead of blaming your failures on your own ineptitude, why not take it to the inherent systemic prejudices of capitalism and the status quo.

Of course, capitalism isn't simply a non-sentient economic concept. No, it is actually run by a secretive group of suits and dark colored turtlenecks who ensure this market-based system continues to exploit and oppress the plebs while funneling undue wealth into their pockets. Can this be fixed with sensible political reforms and policies? No, of course not. As a left-wing extremist, capitalism can only be defeated by overthrowing the existing state and social order. How is this done? With violence and by spray painting the anarchist symbol on walls in alleyways. It has been proven that if a businessman gets a glimpse of a "tagged" building with the anarchist symbol, they burst into flames.

There are plenty of subsets of the left-wing extremist. The most popular is that of the "anti-fascists" or "antifa" as they are more commonly known. Most of the time, these are normal people protesting in the streets. Sometimes they are seen as small well-organized groups who launch violent attacks on political opponents – most notably against Neo-Nazis in Europe.

Figure 15: Capitalism's Kryptonite

There are also animal rights and environmental extremists that offer more nuanced areas for you to conduct violent protests. If you want to fight for Mother Gaia or the rights of a kangaroo to vote in the Australian parliamentary elections, then perhaps you want to put on your PETA sweatshirt and balaclava and raid the animal testing facility to ensure that Maybelline stops their testing of lipstick on farm animals.

There is one finally subgroup of left-wing extremism, that is known as "Autonomists." These are the most violent of the left-wing and reject all forms of external control (e.g., government, societal norms), hence they are super Anarchists. It is twice the violence with only half the underlying philosophy.

X-Games Finalist

You have been riding BMX bikes and skateboards for years now and you want to take it to the extremist level. You have faced off against those naysayers who doubt your abilities for all this time as well. Isn't it time you moved up from the basic bicycle life to the extreme life of an X-games competitor?

This doesn't seem right, there may have been some overlap with the author's next book, *So You Want To Be Paralyzed*. Yep, that is the issue. Although, there is no reason why you cannot be an extreme sports connoisseur as well as a crazed believer who fights against the elitist safety inspectors forcing you to wear pads when you shred. Don't fear the reaper when you rock the half-pipe. Do a kickflip over his head and land on the truth.

OG Extremist

If the new age of extremism isn't whetting your appetite, perhaps you want to go a bit more retro. You don't care for modern conspiracies that any half-wit (or quarter-wit) can come up with in an afternoon. No, you believe in the time-honored conspiracies that have lasted for decades. You believe in the theories that continue to pop up and gain traction in the face of overwhelming scientific evidence. These are the theories that are so far-fetched and devoid of any logic or reason that they just have to be true.

You are an integral part of the zeitgeist. Movies and television have depicted you as wearing tinfoil headgear, living in the desert in a Recreational Vehicle (RV), or wearing a sandwich board sign that says, "The End Is Near" as you yell at people on a busy street in Manhattan. You are the classic extremist, the one who helps others. You stand on the shoulders of giants... well, giant crazies.

VENTURE CAPITAL EXTREMIST

The newest form of extremism may also be the most dangerous. It has emerged from the tech industry. Specifically, this group is composed of right-wing venture capitalists (a fancy word for investor in start-up companies). These "VCs" are very rich, most gained their wealth during the 2001 dot com bubble. The three major figures that you should know – and probably are just sick

Figure 16: Pumping Extremism Before It Was Cool

of hearing of at least one of them by now – are Elon Musk, Peter Thiel, and Marc Andreessen. Now that they have more money than most countries, they have turned their greedy ire toward compromising governments for untold power and even more fucking money. Their ideologies are a swirl of racism, eugenics, and fascism. They are an absolute blast at parties. They believe in – and are working toward – a new tech-billionaire nation-state known as "A Network State." They have already begun implementing this ideology across countries in Latin America, Africa, and Southeast Asia. They believe in the collapse of both the dollar and the current world order hegemon of the United States. The current Vice President of the United States and couch aficionado, JD Vance, is a proponent of these extremists. Other government heads such as Javier Milei in Argentina and Nayib Bukele of El Salvador are backed by these VC extremists. In short, these extremists want to turn the world into a patchwork realm of corporations, even the oceans. Yes, they want to divide and sell off the oceans, probably for their rich deposits of plastic.

PROJECT EXTREME RUNWAY

You have now adopted an extremist label to help identify your level and flavor of crazy, with all the lovely beliefs that come with that. It is time for you to dress the part. We tried to get Tim Gunn to help out, but he told us to fuck off. No matter, this section will help get you set up with the style that matches your new, kooky extremist self.

First, let's define what a cult is exactly. Much like extremism and conspiracy theories, cult is a broad term that includes groups who drink horse medicine all the way to groups who drink poison fruit juice. It is unclear which is worse. Regardless if the followers wear plain white robes or plain black t-shirts, they are devoted to a specific ideology, leader, or belief system. A cult can be based on a religion as well as a political system, a spirituality, a philosophy, a common idea, or even a corporation. For the sake of boundaries, the cults mentioned in this section have additional characteristics that separate them from simply being a "super-fan." This characteristics include:

- Us vs. Them Mentality: Outsiders are dangerous or inferior.

- Distinct Practices: Set of ideas that are vastly different from the mainstream

- Strong Group Identity: Isolation of members from those on the "outside."

Thus, Swifties won't make the cut in the following pages. It was close, though.

CULT CLASSIC

For the more traditional extremist, why not clothe yourself in the classic robes of some of the most famous cults from the past? The use of robes was borrowed from Buddhism, whose followers have worn them for centuries. Newer age cults took these robes – made in the colors of either white, orange, or red. You may also adorn your monochromatic dress with a long, wooden beaded necklace. That is it. No need for underwear or other accoutrements, you would likely need to give those up to the great leader. If you managed to already become the leader, then you are ahead of the game and get to hoard all the undergarments of your followers, you sick freak. Good job! Let's look at a few cults that adopted this classic uniform.

RAJNEESH MOVEMENT

This cult launched itself into the zeitgeist because of folks watching the Netflix documentary, *Wild Wild Country*. Feel free to take a break and watch the 6-part series, that way the author can half-ass this part of the book. The movement was inspired by a professed Indian "mystic" named Bhagwan Shree Rajneesh. No account for creativity in naming his cult.

The cult took up residency in a place that resembled India – rural Oregon. They frowned upon marriage and lived together in a "free love" type of way. Damn hippies. Yet, they also supported contraception and abortion, which is more than can be said of today's right-wing fanatics. Mostly, they just liked having sex and abusing power. A perfect encapsulation of the classic cult.

ORDER OF THE SOLAR TEMPLE

Fly from the western United States across the Atlantic and you come upon an esoteric French cult. This order is best known for the several mass deaths of its members in the mid-1990s. They dressed in white robes with red crosses across the chest, similar to the armor that the Knights Templar wore centuries before. The Order of the Solar Temple claimed lineage to the Knights Templar, so their robes were not a coincidence. They never managed to retrieve the Holy Grail from Indiana Jones either.

This group operated not only in France, but in other French-speaking countries and even made its way to Australia. Nearly 80 people committed mass suicide in two separate occasions in Switzerland. There are worse places to kill yourself, to be fair. Some members shot each other in the head, while most suffocated themselves by putting plastic bags over their heads. This was supposedly to symbolize the ecological disaster that would wipe out the human race in the near future. Joke is on them, for now. The authorities recycled the bags, which were made into happy meal toys at McDonalds.

The founder, Joseph Di Mambro, was a French jeweler who claimed he lived a previous life as a member of the Knights Templar. This is a fairly common tactic by the classic cult leaders, of which you can become one too. The claim of having lived a previous life or multiple previous lives meshes well with dressing in religious garb. So, you will want to increase that crazy of yours and make sure you do a bit of historical research to find your previous self and get those robes flowing free.

Modern Maniac

Maybe the classic robe isn't for you. After all, it can be difficult to accessorize a monochrome robe other than color and a beaded necklace. Perhaps, you want a bit more style with your extremism. You have high-end thoughts and conspiracies about the world. Shouldn't you also have high-end fashion design for your cult, too? You are the modern maniac, but you certainly would not be the only one who preaches a modern form of extremism.

People's Temple

Despite the cult's name, the bizarre rules, and the fact that the founder and leader, Jim Jones, wore a religious robe most of the time, the People's Temple actually encouraged members to attend in casual clothes. This was the 1970s, so you could see members in the modern clothes of the time, such as t-shirts with clever sayings on them and bell-bottom jeans.

The Temple was founded by Jim Jones in the mid-1950s and

was originally more of a form of Christianity with socialist ideals. However, the rules of the cult eventually became ever more arbitrary and "culty" such as it was forbidden to:

- Refuse sex with Jones.
- If you had sex with another member, you had to say that Jim Jones was the best sex you ever had (no, really)
- No drugs, alcohol, or smoking (it was a very fit group of cultists)
- Behavior associated with capitalist habits (No Solar Temple McDonald's toys for them)

By the mid-1970s, the group had moved to a compound in Guyana, South America, aptly named "Jonestown." In 1978, the group ordered all its members to drink toxic Kool-Aid, committing a mass suicide of 918 people, over 200 of them being children. This is where the term "Drinking the Kool Aid" originated. The Kool Aid Man survived the suicide by bursting through a wall at the compound to escape.

NXIVM

Pronounced "Nexium," like the drug, this cult sprung up in 1998 and became popular in the last few years after a famous actress from the show *Smallville*, Allison Mack, was found guilty of racketeering with the group.

The group gained followers by promoting itself with Executive Success Seminars, led by a man named Keith Raniere. In fact, NXIVM was at first a company that focused on self-help. And what was Keith's clothing of choice? He wore a sleek collared shirt often with a modern sweater over top and glasses. Keith looked more like a Silicon Valley CEO than a cult leader. Although, the difference between those two types of people is miniscule.

Allison Mack and others aggressively recruited young women as members, who would be coerced into providing nude photographs or other incriminating material. This material was then used as blackmail to force the women to have sex with Keith. NXIVM even tried to recruit Emma Watson and Kelly Clarkson. It was also alleged that they would brand members like cattle, which a lot of Silicon Valley companies do, too.

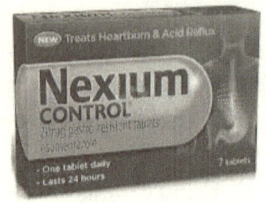

RAËLISM

Figure 17: NXIVM cult was all about control of your mind and your heartburn.

In 1973, Claude Vorilhon claimed he was contacted by an advanced extraterrestrial race called the Elohiim. This UFO-based cult was founded a year later with Claude serving as a near-Messianic figure who had exclusive knowledge that the Elohim created humanity through genetic engineering. They must have taken the day off when designing the human back.

When you mention an UFO-based cult, you assume you are going to get wild, batshit beliefs. That is very presumptuous of you. It is correct, though. Members are encouraged to cut ties, embrace sexual liberation such as polyamory, and exploit females to prepare for the arrival of the Elohim. Basically, it is like the book/Netflix show, *The Three Body Problem*, but with a bit more sexual exploitation. The original logo of the group was a Nazi swastika within a Star of David, so clearly drugs are not outlawed (they have since changed the symbol).

The Raëlists have made wild scientific claims, including in 2002 when they said they had cloned a human named Eve (how original). They also require members to give large financial sums to help build an embassy for the Elohim's return to Earth. No visible progress of this embassy has been documented and they still haven't renewed the author's visa application.

Blue Oyster Cult

Formed in 1967 outside of New York, their name was inspired by an alien conspiracy. They engaged in rituals that often required the follower to stand up to the Reaper itself. But you don't need to fear him.

Aluminum Avant Garde

Besides flowing robes, there may not be anything else as recognizable for conspiracy theorists and extremists as the aluminum foil hat. It actually has a longer history than you might think, tracing its roots back to a short story from 1927 called *The Tissue-Culture King*. The powers of the hat are supposed to protect the wearer from government mind control or electromagnetic waves. The beauty of the tin foil hat is that you can mold it into different styles, not just the traditional one with a pointy top. Go turn your conspiracy into art. You can protect yourself from deadly government rays while creating aesthetically innovative art that goes against the establishment. Tin foil hats are just the tip of the...well, of the tin foil hat. There are cults that have taken their wardrobe to new artistic highs or lows.

Heaven's Gate

Probably one of the more (if not most) far out cult movements of the 20th century is Heaven's Gate. It was founded in the mid 1970s combining new age religion with a firm belief in aliens. Basically, it was Scientology before Scientology was cool. The founders, Marshall Applewhite and Bonnie Nettles, met in the early 70s, in which Bonnie had said that their meeting was foretold to her by aliens. They didn't bother with wading into crazy like most cults, they dove into the deep end. Actually they dove into the shallow end and hit their head on the pool floor, which explains a lot.

The group recruited members for a few years before retreating into reclusiveness, banning sex and drugs – which, honestly, what is even the point of the joining the cult then? In terms of cult clothing, the 39 remaining members in the 1990s wore identical black shirts and sweatpants, but most impressively, each had their own set of new black-and-white Nike Decades sneakers. Finally, they all wore identical armbands that said, "Heaven's Gate Away Team." They would go on to lose all but 6 games in their inaugural NBA season.

In 1996, the members completed a mass suicide. They each lied under purple shrouds and drank a cocktail of barbiturates and alcohol – so drugs seemed to be back on the table by then.

PODCAST POSH WEAR

Recently, cult-like groups have sprung up around television and podcast personalities. The cults of the past are gone, members have traded in white robes and drug-laced juice for muscle shirts and bullshit vitamin supplements. This has been dubbed the "Alt-Right Pipeline," which is where the consistent consuming of more right-wing political contact (such as anti-woke) gradually exposes a person to ever more radical right-wing content until they find themselves storming a government building. Key figures who fit into this mold include Ben Shapiro, Charlie Kirk, and Jordan Peterson. Their arguments seem almost reasonable and thoughtful at times, but underneath they pitch or give voices to the far more radical parts of their beliefs. We have met a few of these characters already, but you can dive a bit deeper into them now.

Joe Rogan is the equivalent of a gateway drug to the Alt-Right movement. He is like the diet coke to Alex Jones, complete with the black t-shirt. Except where Alex Jones looks like a metastasized tumor, Joe is often associated with UFC events and workout supplements.

Joe started as the host of the show, *Fear Factor,* where contestants would be forced to eat cockroaches. So Joe comes from a prestigious background, fully qualified to give credence to political and social issues as well as synthetic Human Growth Hormone (HGH) supplements. They go hand-in-hand. He does this on his weekly podcast, *The Joe Rogan Experience*, which he has hosted since 2009. Finish off your Joe Rogan-esque look with terrible tattoos on your arms and a "bubble gut" that comes from abuse of hormones and supplements. You'll look like a lower-case letter B, isn't that cool, bro?

Once you have graduated from Joe Rogan and the other alt-right podcasters, you'll be in the Infowars zone with Alex Jones, who you are familiar with already.

Alex Jones's Infowars is a media platform that he has used rather successfully to push his conspiracy theories and his line of bogus vitamin supplements and other merchandise [More on this in Chapter 8]. His clothing choice is simpler – a black t-shirt and jeans. This is his way to connect

Figure 18: Peak fitness of the extremist takes time, money, and determinism.

with the common man – and that is literal, for his audience is almost exclusively straight white males who are not college-educated. In addition to his simple attire, Jones tends to sport a beard, mostly to hide his overly puffy, alcoholic face.

Which goes to show that if you go down the podcast route, you may find yourself chugging protein shakes, HGH, and light beers to get that elite physique like Alex.

TRUTHER CHIC

Last, and certainly least, the online cults of the present day. The basement-dwelling troglodytes have risen in popularity over the last decade, utilizing the deep, dark corners of the Internet to recruit, complain, and theorize. While most hide behind troll faces, memes, and anonymous screennames, they do sometimes pop their heads out in public and show off their wardrobes.

QAnon

As mentioned earlier, the leader of QAnon, Ron Watkins, dresses like a strange 90s kid, showing up in plenty of plaid and sporting a creepy moustache and "soul patch." However, the QAnon traditional dress is wrapped in an American flag and was best seen when these January 6th truthers stormed the United States Capitol.

The truthers and QAnon believed that the 2020 election was stolen by the Democrats and Joseph R. Biden. They based this on the evidence…wait, there wasn't any evidence. So, they based this on…their feelings, which is funny since they hate those. Regardless, these "people" decided to storm the United States Capitol to tell Congress there who were trying to validate the election that they were totally wrong and deserved to be hung outside like it was late 18th century France. Which is funny since they probably hate the French for not being true Americans.

These "totally innocent protestors and visitors" as the right-wing considered them, came in all shapes, sizes, and colors. Well, maybe not colors. They did sport plenty of red, white, and blue though.

If you want to go the ultimate "patriot" route, then you want to dress in truther chic. It comes with such varieties as:

- Shamanistic: Yes, the popular "QAnon Shaman is a trendsetter, utilizing face paint, a hat made of yak tusks, and no shirt anywhere to be found.

- Full Metal Jackass: Yes, there were several January 6thers that wore full military or S.W.A.T.-esque gear complete with zip-ties to kidnap Congresspeople.

- Klassic Karen: There was plenty of red, white, and pinkers at the Capitol, screaming and complaining as Karens do with more than a hint of antisemitism.

- <u>MAGA Cowboy:</u> Perhaps you want to invoke a Western sensibility with a cowboy hat, spurs, and a whole lot of MAGA merch and Trump flags. Wave it proudly.

- <u>Bearded Loser:</u> You could just come in your normal QAnon basement-wear, sweatpants, long hair, uncut beard, and the smell of a thousand showers not taken.

The choices for how you can dress are nearly limitless – as long as you never dress like a normal person. But you aren't normal anymore, you are quickly on your way to becoming a full extremist. You are now ready to stand out from the crowd. Now that you have your attire, you need your admirers. It is time to fill your toolbelt of truth to attract the fringes and hopefully some of the masses to your fledgling cause.

Expose what they won't let us say...

B *I* <u>U</u>

Free your truth NOW 📢

Connections 3,987,911,321   Most connected ⬇⬆

 **ShadowSignal** ✓ 6h ago

Wake up, sheeple! Yes, the 5G towers are powered by vibe-shifts from Area 51, but who really controls the "lizard people" (Canadians). That's why maple syrup doesn't have TARIFFS, because of Israel, who started Ukraine. (It's all science until it isn't). DON'T TAKE THE VACCINE.

📢 66
Exposed

CHAPTER 6

TOOLS OF THE TRADE

"Those who can make people believe absurdities, can make people commit atrocities."

— VOLTAIRE, BROKEN FRENCH AIR CONDITIONING UNIT

I t is time to spread your message, recruit your followers, and fully take charge of your extremism. You will need a set of tools to do all of these activities. In this chapter, we will deep dive into these tools and how you can effectively use them to build your extremism empire.

MISSUS INFORMATION

The fabrication of information is far from new. Records of misinformation and disinformation can be traced back to at least the Roman era. Octavian (who would become Augustus, the first emperor of Rome) printed witty slogans on coins that spread lies about his rival, Marc Antony. This would be the equivalent of misleading social media posts that we see so often today. Although, you have to admit, printing them on a coin is far more badass than simply tweeting 240 characters. Notably, Octavian printed coins that said Antony was a womanizer and a drunk, who was corrupted by Cleopatra. He also said that Antony totally had a foot fetish. Not that there is anything wrong with that. In fact, most extremists have some sort of fetish, why not feet?

However, printing memes on coins can be cumbersome and does get expensive, you are printing this stuff on currency after all. The misinformation game changed in 1493, when the Gutenberg printing press was invented, allowing for relatively faster spreading of information – fake or otherwise. Of course, it wasn't too effective at first because most people couldn't read anyway, and Gutenberg only had a select few emoji stamps he could use in those days.

As literacy rates rose across the world except for in the deep south of the United States, so did the presence of fake news, misinformation, and hoaxes. Most notably, "The Great Moon Hoax" of 1835, where the *New York Sun* newspaper published several articles claiming that life was discovered on the Moon. The articles came with illustrations of human-like bat creatures and blue unicorns. People fell for this, somehow. Perhaps it could be true if we ever get to the moon, since we have only been able to fake it so far.

Outside of more lighthearted hoaxes like the Great Moon Hoax, misinformation took on more serious affairs such as wars, conflicts, politics, and environmental catastrophes. These have obviously carried over tenfold in today's world of increased social media and dearth of critical thinking. Exactly the two things you can take advantage of to further your own causes and associated hoaxes. This is the world of troll armies, ultra memes, sock-puppet networks, and little-to-no fact-checking by a large faction of people.

MEME ME UP, SCOTTY

Memes have been around long before the Internet. Linguists have claimed that humans have used the concept of memes for centuries to communicate as they are shortcuts for sharing information across society. The term "meme" has been used as early as the 1940s but the definition as we know it is attributed to the famous scientist, Richard Dawkins in his 1976 book, *The Selfish Gene*. He called it, "The smallest unit of sound in speech." In the simplest explanation, a meme can be defined as a self-replicating piece of information. Something gets stuck in your head like a song or a joke, and then you repeat it to friends. That is a meme. We humans love to repeat things, which is the replication aspect of the meme.

Nowadays, when you think of a meme, your mind most likely conjures up your elderly parent sharing a picture with a few words of text over it on Facebook. It usually takes a complex topic and boils it down to a barely understandable joke. That is exactly what you want to utilize in mass to sway people to your view. Your basic meme has a few words of top text and a few words of bottom text over a generic picture. There are several keys to making an effective extremist meme:

1. Simplify: Don't overthink the meme, you can always make more on the same topic. The point is to take a complicated, nuanced topic and strip away any thoughtfulness.

2. Mischaracterize: This means to take things out of context, which should be easy as a meme has no context to explain the points you make in the text.

3. Exaggerate: Hyperbole is your friend, whatever the original fact (if there even is one) is, you should ensure that your meme makes a mountain out of a mole hill.

4. Incite: Finally, be sure you pack in as much angry rhetoric as possible into the subtext of your meme. You want to get people on your side riled up and at the same time anger the other, reasonable side of the

argument. Always argue in bad faith, and memes allow you to do that easily for any issue.

IN TOO DEEP

The term "deepfake" is a combination of "deep," which refers to the Artificial Intelligence (AI) technology used to create "fake" content. The earliest use of the term came on a Reddit webpage aptly termed "deepfakes" in 2017. At that time, it was used for productive content, mostly to put celebrity faces onto pornographic videos. You know, the stuff that moves society forward.

Today, deepfakes are widespread across pictures, videos, and recorded speeches. Notable deepfakes have included a picture of the Pope in a gangster puffy jacket, a video of Queen Elizabeth II dancing, or Donald Trump in a scuffle with the local police. Of course, none of these actually happened – although it is up in the air about the Queen's dance video. The deepfake technology has become so advanced and ubiquitous, that companies are emerging that use AI to help determine whether a piece of media content is real or fake. Almost any person with half a brain and a whole computer can create deepfakes easily, even you!

There are plenty of free software versions available to start creating extremist content. The only limit is your imagination and perhaps, eventually, laws against creating and distributing the content. They would have to know it was you though. There are millions of different iterations you can choose from so get producing those deepfakes. Flood the Internet until no one can tell what is real or what isn't.

TELEGRAM CRACKER

One of the extremist's best friends is Telegram. It was created in 2013 by two Russian brothers, Nikolai and Pavel Durov. As a messenger application with end-to-end encryption (i.e., whatever you send is protected by computer code from being revealed), it was touted as a safe place for conservative, right-wing content, which is not only accepted but encouraged. It has nearly a billion active monthly users, touting it as a place to express true freedom. It's like if a bunch of racist teenagers ran WhatsApp. Similar to the Dark Web, with Telegram you can get anything you want. People use the application to buy and sell weapons, illicit drugs, and engage in prostitution, among other things. And while the Dark Web is notoriously difficult for your average user to find and navigate, Telegram makes it easy so even 13-year-old Johnny can express ship himself an AR-15 and a handful of gummy LSD. Boy, what a field trip he is going to have.

When you are not buying and selling all things illegal, you can join and chat with your fellow domestic terrorists, or international ones, it is a global application after all. ISIS has used Telegram for recruiting purposes. It is a hotbed for extremism. In 2023, over 59 million pieces of extremist content were removed from the application. So, there is still room for growth when you join.

In the United States, domestic terrorist groups have utilized Telegram to spout their ideologies and sometimes, their manifestos. Post-COVID and with the rise of QAnon, the number of hate groups that had private channels grew to nearly 50. Because of its encryption and dedication to freedom of expression, Telegram is your best place to start recruiting with a lower possibility of getting caught. Although, some people have been so don't consider it a complete safe haven. However, regardless of the bad luck of some extremists, you can utilize coded messaging (discussed later in this chapter) to help bring in interested parties and use private chats (harder to trace) to bring them fully into your cause with more direct messaging. Because the average user on Telegram in the United States is angry, young, and conservative, your best bet is to cater to their anger when constructing and posting your extremist views.

Gabulous

If you are looking at catering to the extreme far-right for your recruiting, then there is one other software platform that can be of use. Yes, Twitter (X) has unofficially become a safe haven for the far-right due to the expert handling of its CEO, Elon Musk. The Muskrat has worked tirelessly (probably not) to not only tank the value of the billion-dollar platform, but also to make it friendly to far-right extremists. However, there is another Skywalker.

If you haven't already, meet Gab. Founded in 2016 as an alternative to Facebook and Twitter, it has emphasized its commitment to free speech. Just like with Telegram, billing yourself as a bastion of free speech inevitably means that you will happily host extremist and hateful content. And boy, does Gab deliver. Based on a study by the Pew Center, Gab is the only alternative content site that had no examples of offensive or harassing content being moderated or removed. Gab's CEO states that users can moderate the content themselves, which is the equivalent of letting monkeys run the zoo, really, really racist monkeys. Which means it is a very useful tool for recruiting new members to your cause. For example, in September 2017, following the United the Right rally in Charlottesville that ignited into political violence, Gab experienced an increase of over 3,300 users. There still remains less than a million users on the social media platform, but what it lacks in quantity makes up for in quality extremists.

XTREME TWEETS

Elon Musk has made Twitter (X) into a haven for the far-right. The previous two books in this series have extensively covered Twitter, so this section will be short. Dictators use it to quash uprisings, oligarchs use it (or buy it) to change the algorithms to their will. And wouldn't you know it, extremists all over the world use it to blast out their messaging, recruit others, and just generally be a pain in the ass to the rest of the population.

At this point, you should know how to use it. It is 280 characters of pure vitriol and hatred. With the new algorithms in place, even new users without any connection to your cause, will eventually be recommended to follow you and others. An online content user tested this theory out by creating a blank user with simple interests and within days was recommended content by Elon Musk, Laura Loomer, and other far-right accounts. It has become incredibly easy with the new algorithms and AI integrated into the platform, so don't waste any time. Set up an account, follow as many far-right posts as you can, and produce your own hateful content to gain followers – both online and offline. Show everyone what the X really means.

Truthiness

The last – and certainly least – technology tool that will be of use to your extremist recruiting is TruthSocial, the social media platform created by Donald Trump. As of this writing, TruthSocial still exists and can be utilized, although it has crashed in value at an alarming rate. Like most Trump enterprises – steaks, vodka, casinos – it will eventually have to declare bankruptcy and be shut down. But for now, it is still around and thus is a great option for you to connect with the MAGA crowd.

It was launched in February 2022 utilizing another social media's code (Mastodon) as its foundation. TruthSocial struggled to find footing at first – and notably still struggles – as it was not available on most application downloading sites. Its competition remains Gab and Parler (another conservative social media platform that doesn't even deserve a section). The entire concept of TruthSocial came to be because Donald Trump was banned from Facebook and Twitter in 2021. His ban was lifted in 2022 following a bizarre online poll conducted by Elon Musk.

TruthSocial is great to promote far-right ideals and extremist leanings. Even better is that they work to remove dissenting opinions to the far-right, so no one can contradict you ever. Hard to beat that type of publicity. In 2022, ProPublica found that TruthSocial moderators would shadowban (banning a user without the user knowing) liberal and progressive users and content. So you can safely use this tool for recruiting without all those pesky facts and well-researched evidence to get in your way and in the way of the less-than-critical thinking skills of your potential online flock.

Tune In, Turn Out

If you have read the previous books in this series, then you can recall a section on podcasts in the Turing Award Winner, *So You Want To Be An Oligarch*. As useful as podcasts are for generating people to buy your shit [more on this in Chapter 8], they have become another great technological avenue for spewing hateful rhetoric or sharing dog whistles. This isn't a new concept as AM radio, with hosts like Rush Limbaugh, perfected the concept

Figure 19: Rush Limbaugh was the original fat, angry, conspiracy theorist on the radio waves.

of conservative talk radio to rile up the masses and spread conspiracy theories or false information. Podcasts just made it even easier to access more people.

The key here is that you need a bit of finesse and subtlety. There aren't too many (at least popular) extremist podcasts that you will find on Spotify. You'll want to slog your way through a few episodes of podcasts like "The Joe Rogan Experience," "The Jordan B. Peterson podcast," and Steve Bannon's War Room podcast" to get a feel for the tone and content you want to share. These podcasts, and similar ones, take the libertarian route of freedom of speech and seek to give everyone a fair opportunity to express their opinions. Unfortunately, after having to listen to even a fraction of this dribble, you'll realize that they often give more leeway to conspiracies and dubious iconoclasts without any serious fact-checking. Thus, they inadvertently (or perhaps purposefully) give validation to far-fetched ideas and fringe thinking. This, in turn, opens the door to people to explore the fringe and beyond it. It usually is a gateway drug of extremism, which can get people hooked on the idea of questioning every-thing, even without attempting to fact check or provide evidence.

This is the strategy you can employ on your podcast, if you

choose. Get people interested in a popular medium in what seems like a moderate setting, only to provide fodder for extremism and push more susceptible people toward other platforms and ideas. So, turn those microphones on and start preaching to the impressionable masses. Who knows, maybe you'll be the Ira Glass of extremism.

It's Just A Game, Bro

The last tool in the technology sphere is the gaming platform. Whether it is Twitch, Discord, or something similar, tapping into the angry, young white men who dominate the space is key to increasing your extremist foothold. In the Academy Award Winner For Best Original Song, *So You Want To Be A Dictator*, we discussed Twitch and how politicians used it for garnering support and funding for charity, so we won't belabor the topic here. Know that Twitch is a great way to mask your extremism and utilize people's love of watching others play video games (for some reason) to start spouting your views and get people's curiosity of extremist piqued. You should look at violent video games like *Call of Duty* (CoD), which favors wannabe gun-toting young boys who only need a little push to move toward extremist views. For this segment, let's focus on Discord as it has been at the forefront of news in the last few years for harboring users and channels of users who spout extremism, share military secrets, or trade weird anime memes. Pick your poison.

In 2021, the European Union released a report on the growing concern and connection between video games and violent extremism. Discord is known as a "game adjacent" platform, meaning it doesn't host video games but is used by gamers to chat while playing. Since its inception in the mid-2010s, it has branched out beyond video games and is used by millions to simply chat about common interests. Channels are set up where users can be invited to join and share content. Users can also privately message each other, which is very hard to record and track by authorities. Thus, it has become a breeding ground for violent extremist movements and until recently, went largely unmoderated or had users "self-moderate," which as we mentioned early, works surprisingly poorly. Who knew?

Discord is a great avenue for you to work on what has been called "extremist cybergrooming" because the platform is used extensively by teenagers. Those wonderfully impressionable youngsters who have developed complex emotions that they don't understand how to deal with yet. That is a jackpot for you. The key is to setup channels that follow the policy guidelines (perhaps a generic conservative one) or one that is just vaguely xenophobic. Then you can privately message new users to work on sharing your more extremist beliefs in a safe space (the irony is not lost here). You can also join channels that are on the fringe, whether it is political, social, music-related, or of course violent video games to tap into that bloodlust. You can then start to groom users in there and get them to your Discord safe spaces for further indoctrination. Be careful, as Discord has started to get more aggressive at policing its servers, but there is risk when you are mining a vein this rich in potential extremism. And your parents said that games would rot your brain, well, you can make that a reality for others!

Zip Code

You may have heard of coded messaging. Another name for it in politics is a "dog whistle." This is where you use suggestive language to garner support for a particular group without provoking others to oppose what you said. It is named after the concept of a dog whistle that plays at an ultrasonic decibel level that only dogs can hear.

Extremists love to use coded messaging to promote their views to a wider audience and hopefully recruit people who recognize the underlying message. The dog whistle is a great tool for your extremist arsenal, and it can be paired with any of the previous technologies discussed. In fact, you'll want to as your audience is mostly online these days. But where to start? Here are a few examples of popular dog whistles:

- "<u>Family Values</u>" – Often used to imply opposition to LGTBQ+ rights and support of traditional gender roles. The politicians that use this more often than not end up being discovered in a sex scandal (or two) and the irony is always lost on them.

- "<u>Law and Order</u>" – Frequently used to appeal to votes concerned about crime but usually carries racial undertones. Those who use this phrase tend to side with the police in any and all matters, particularly when they murder an innocent Black person, which ya know, is like all the time. "Back the Blue" is also a newer form of this sentiment.

- "<u>Welfare Queens</u>" – This retro term was popularized by Ronald Reagan to evoke stereotypes about Blacks and poverty without directly mentioning race. Ain't Reagan grand? At least he gave out jellybeans.

- "<u>Inner City</u>" – Used to refer to urban areas with high populations of People of Color, usually implying crime and poverty while – again – not mentioning race. "Urban" is also often used in a negative context in the same manner. Nowadays, the conservative right basically lumps anyone who even drove through a city as part of this urban decay of American society.

- "<u>88</u>" – This is more common in far-right circles of Europe (Germany and Austria in particular) that is used by Neo Nazis to communicate with each other. "H" is the 8th letter of the alphabet and so two together represents HH or "Heil Hitler." Pretty efficient dog whistle, guess that is why it's German.

- "<u>Save the Children</u>" – Yes, this is actually the name of a well-known anti-poverty charity. Unfortunately, those noble souls over at QAnon decided to adopt the slogan, putting it on t-shirts and bumper stickers, which is a coded message about the vast conspiracy of pedophiles and child abductors in power – mostly on the left.

- "Immigrant/Migrant" – These are interchangeable depending on where you live. The entire aspect of immigration is used as a dog whistle and a lightning rod extensively in the United States and Europe. In the United States, these terms are used to represent basically all of Central and South America...and the Caribbean...and the Middle East, and Europe. Hell, some people are even attacking the Irish, who really haven't immigrated to the U.S. in mass since the 19th century. While in Europe, where migrant is the favored term, it could represent Islamophobia, anti-Africa, anti-Eastern Europe, or just all-around xenophobia.

- Emojis – Yep, dog whistlers have coopted several emojis to help spread their messages while avoiding content moderation rules. Finally, the eggplant emoji comes in handy for more than just casual hookups. Anti-vaccine groups on Meta have been using the cake emoji, which stands for "eaten the cake" and refers to users who have taken vaccines (not just COVID-19). Users will sometimes indicate that someone has taken three or four "slices" of Pfizer or Moderna. They also sometimes use the Pizza Emoji to dress up the same coded messaging. A cheese pizza, as mentioned earlier in this book, also represented CP or Child Porn and the conspiracy that Democrats had locked up kids in a pizza parlor basement. The cheese pizza emoji is still being used to bolster offshoots of that original theory in QAnon online circles across social media platforms.

These are but a mere sampling of the many different dog whistles available for you to co-opt. The previous examples give you a mostly complete look into how secretive and thus, how useful coded messaging can be. It will be helpful in the spreading of your messages – discreetly – both online and offline. As your extremist movement grows, so will your toolbelt of dog whistles that you can use, update, and reuse. There are still plenty of emojis that can be co-opted too – try the spaghetti one.

Shed a Tear

Start practicing for that Oscar speech, or in this case, your bizarre rambling about your manifesto and the state of the world. Yes, crying like a little bitch is a great way to feign anger and fan the flames of hatred toward a specific group or event. A lot of people believe it and see it as fierce passion for the subject. The most infamous at this feat is none other than Alex Jones, the giant tumor of extremism and host of InfoWars. Jones is perpetually red-in-the-face, but he often breaks out the waterworks when talking about a conspiracy theory that he is pushing at the moment. (For example, the Sandy Hook Massacre). This is your chance to work on your acting while recruiting more people to your cause who are as passionate about extremism as you appear to be.

Plead the Fifth

Lawyers! Yes, a team of lawyers is something you will eventually have to fully invest in as you grow your extremist movement. This is because you will be skirting around and bumping up against slander and libel laws as you hone your skills at spewing hateful rhetoric and dubious conspiracy claims. Alex Jones, Fox News, and Rush Limbaugh had to utilize legal teams when they got into trouble regarding particular events [More on this in Chapter 7]. Just as a refresher, you should know the difference between slander and libel when it comes to defamation:

- <u>Slander</u> – Oral or spoken communication, so basically if you make a YouTube video discussing how Harry Styles is a devil-worshipping rapist and baby hippo murderer, you would be liable to be sued by him.

- <u>Libel</u> – This is communication by writing or graphic. So if you create a picture of Harry Styles eating baby hippos like in the adjacent picture, then you will be liable to be sued by him.

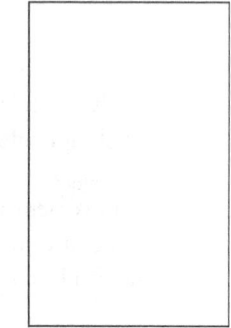

Figure 20: Yeah, No Thanks. Nice Try.

Easy as that, so be careful and choose your words wisely (dog whistles!), but more importantly have a lawyer on retainer for when you eventually do screw up. It happens to all extremists, it's a rite of passage.

GISH, GIRL

If you have ever been involved in debate club, then good for you, nerd. For those of us that missed that nonstop thrill ride, there is a particular rhetorical technique that can be used to win. A debater floods their opponent with a succession of arguments, regardless if they are accurate or even relevant to the topic. This is the Gish gallop. It was perfected by Duane Gish, a creationist who used this tactic in debates against evolutionary scientists to win...or at least not lose. This has been co-opted by more extremist influencers in the modern day. The core idea behind Gish gallop – and why it is so effective – is that the opponent is forced to spend valuable time refuting all the arguments. It can give the impression that the Gish galloper has a stronger case, but who is really just spraying a firehose of information. Remember, always put the burden of proof on the other person. Forcing them to disprove one of your claims is very difficult to do. You can utilize this to flood followers who will be too overwhelmed to question you. You can also use it against naysayers who may try to convince others that you are wrong.

By utilizing and combining these tools to their fullest, you can quickly push out your extremist beliefs, recruit others to your budding movement, and get them to fight for you (at least online). Now you have everything you need to organically grow your extremist movement and become a powerful leader. But there are moments – events – in time that can lead to massive shifts in beliefs, politics, and overall perspectives. You will learn how you can exploit these events in the next chapter to amplify your message.

Stand up, be heard!

B *I* U

Join the struggle

Outrage 6198   Most in-perspective ↓↑

EndOppressionBy11 ✓ 2 days ago

If your smoothie isn't certified union-made by a insect-centric co-op of non-hierarchical bees, then you're LITERALLY contributing to GENOCIDE.

 9112
Allies

CHAPTER 7

A CRISIS AND AN OPPORTUNITY

"Never let a good crisis go to waste."

— WINSTON CHURCHILL, PICKLED PRIME
MINISTER

There is a famous quote attributed to Albert Einstein (or paraphrased from an ancient Chinese proverb, take your pick), that says "In the midst of every crisis, lies great opportunity." It is time to explore these opportunities. Because in each crisis also lies the fog of truth, untapped anger, and that sweet, sweet exploitation. Yes, in this chapter, you will learn about some of the most famous and horrific events of the past decades that spirited extremists utilized to push their own conspiracy theories, sell products, or just drum up general outrage. It is a delicate balance as you have to exploit the crisis without getting into any legal trouble. Come and take a walk down opportunity lane.

The Populist Crew

A populist is typically a politician but can be anyone who blames elitist groups for the problems and challenges of ordinary people. Thus, they tend to cater to the common person with their anti-establishment views. Populist movements are usually anti-intellectual and have a general disdain towards experts and the well-educated. Populism tends to be the final stage before full-blown extremism. You are getting an advanced degree with this book straight to extremism, but it is important to know what comes beforehand. In fact, when it comes to exploiting crises, you may want to begin with more populist statements that blame the tragic event on a more abstract thing, such as the rich elites, minorities, or a concept like Capitalism or Communism.

These topics are usually already despised or untrusted by your average John or Jane Q. Public. So, when a crisis hits that can be blamed on one of these things, it provides you with the opportunity to nurture public dissatisfaction with the status quo.

The formula for exploiting a crisis to your own extremist movement is fairly straightforward. First, start with a recent event that people perceive as a failure, perhaps of security. For example, a school shooting would be seen as a failure on the part of an authority that let the horrific event happen. You need to increase your rhetoric at this first stage, perhaps frame it as an example of flaws in the current system and its ruling elites. Or blame the cause on the rise of minority groups and refugees. Now, exercise those acting skills (crying, forced anger) and create a greater sense of crisis within the crisis. A horrible shooting or devastating environmental event actually is far worse than the single event as it blows open all the problems with the current system or status quo. Now, old and new followers are very concerned about the recent event and get increasingly angry and scared like you pretend to be. You've got their full attention, open up the extremist hose to full stream and share other conspiracies, dive deeper into the current event and how it is connected to other ideas you have. Seize this opportunity. Let's take a look at recent events where others have seized their opportunity.

It Takes Two, Towers

It is hard to look further than probably the granddaddy of all conspiracy theories for its scope and staying power, 9/11. We have already discussed the conspiracy theory surrounding that day in 2001, but let's look at how others have exploited the tragedy and its associated conspiracy theories.

It has been over twenty years, and despite extensive reports by the U.S. government's 9/11 commission, U.S. government agencies, and expert groups refuting the existence of any hidden conspiracy, many believers forge on. The reason they do so is because 9/11 is the perfect vehicle to lead people into the idea of a Deep State. The 9/11 Truth Movement started soon after the attacks and during the subsequent investigations. They claimed the facts had been hidden by the government. They stated that thousands of people who were involved in the rescue, cleanup, and victims of the attacks were all in on the conspiracy to help George W. Bush enter a war in the Middle East for oil. Most people can barely keep from telling you spoilers to the latest television show, so the claim that thousands have been keeping it a secret for years is Simone Biles levels of mental gymnastics.

Other conspiracy and extremist movements have co-opted the ideas from the 9/11 Truth Movement to gain new followers. The Deep State is a theme that we have seen (and will continue to see) woven across many of these terrible events. They are the boogeyman that is easy to point the finger at and blame. The falsehoods of 9/11 mesh well with recent online movements like QAnon about the belief that global elites are working toward curtailing civil liberties in response to an event – in this case the attacks – to facilitate the establishment of an authoritarian world government. The lesson here is that 9/11 is basically the bread and butter of exploiting a crisis for extremist gain. Its conspiracy theories are so well thought out and extensive that it gives the appearance of detailed detective work regardless of any basis on any sort of scientific fact. Extremists continue to utilize it to gain new followers and so should you. They say, "Jet fuel cannot melt steel beams" and you say "9/11 can certainly melt a few minds."

Hook, Line, Sinker

On December 14, 2012, a 20-year-old white man, after killing his mother at their home in Newtown, Connecticut, broke into Sandy Hook Elementary School and killed 26 people. 20 of the victims were second graders between six and seven years old. The perpetrator, Adam Lanza, shot himself in the head before he could be captured. It is the deadliest shooting in Connecticut's history and renewed the debate on gun control laws and mental health in the United States, which was promptly solved by politicians and there haven't been any troubles since. Except for like, hundreds more mass shootings since then, but who is counting anymore? Seriously, who is counting?

This tragic event caused lasting damage to families and for the country as a whole. However, for some, it was an opportunity to spread conspiracy theories about the event and increase their own popularity – or notoriety in this case – at the expense of the victims. Just another average day in America.

While there are fringe actors who have cast doubt on what occurred at Sandy Hook, there is really only one name you need to know associated with this event. Alex Jones, who you have read about several times so far, is the main character of this exploitation.

Although the conspiracy theory was started by other fringe characters, it was Alex who popularized the notion that the massacre at the elementary school never happened. He denied the shooting occurred and instead claimed it was a "classified training exercise" created by federal and local law enforcement with help from the news media. The most egregious claim was that he called the parents and the children at the school "crisis actors." You read that right, Alex thought that the dead children were simply actors. They probably had Screen Actors Guild (SAG) cards stashed in their pencil cases.

The concept of this theory was based on a shooting drill in Iowa, known as "Operation Closed Campus," which was subsequently cancelled before ever being exercised. This initial theory that Alex Jones spouted led to offshoot theories. One of these concluded that Sandy Hook was a false flag operation staged by the government to force politicians to push through new gun control legislation. It does seem like the government could have found an easier way to do that rather than shooting up a bunch of kids. However, it can be difficult to push through bills in today's gridlocked Congress. Just like the 9/11 Truthers, this idea again touches on the Deep State mentality where the government controls everything, including shootings at public elementary schools.

In 2019, Alex Jones recanted his stance and stated that the massacre at Sandy Hook was real. Although this was less about him growing a conscience and more that the parents of the children sued him for $1 billion (yes with a B). In 2022, the jury subsequently ordered Jones to pay the full amount as part of three defamation (remember that word?) lawsuits. Jones even tried crying on the jury stand to get out of the suit, which obviously did not work.

During this decade-long fiasco, Jones gained popularity among the fringe and extremists of the country. He used this to make lots of money on selling products [More on this in Chapter 8] and to keep up his loyal following. There are two lessons here, the first is that using the false flag route is a good tragedy strategy to gain followers and get your message out there through provocation. The second lesson is that you have to be careful with that pesky defamation aspect. Despite the United States barely giving two shits about mass shootings these days, the victims and their lawyers won't be so blase if you push it too far like Jones did. Talk about a misfire.

Capitol Gains

On January 6th, 2021, a mob of supporters for U.S. President Donald Trump attacked the U.S. Capitol building in Washington, D.C. in an attempted coup. Or it was a peaceful demonstration depending on who you ask. The rioters trashed many offices of politicians and five people ended up dead, including a police officer. Despite the entire event being televised in its entirety by news stations and a bevy of pictures and cell phone video from members of the mob, there are still people who claim it was a false flag operation. In this case, the culprit of this supposed operation is the Federal Bureau of Investigation (FBI) according to Donald Trump and former Republican presidential candidate, Vivek Ramaswamy. It seems to have worked as according to a January 2024 poll by the University of Maryland, 25 percent of Americans say it is "probably" or "definitely" true that the FBI instigated the January 6th attack. Republicans come in at 34 percent who believe that the FBI organized and encouraged the insurrection. 13 percent of Democrats believe this theory as well. The conclusion is that people are idiots who will believe anything. This is yet another example of blaming a horrific event on the government. This one is especially interesting because the event is so well recorded. People will still think it was a coordinated effort by the higher powers that be. Perhaps, if you get a big enough movement, you can give storming the Capitol (or whichever government building tickles your fancy) another go. After all, you can just get yourself a pardon. As they say, if you don't succeed, storm, storm again.

Pandemic Profits

You have read at length about COVID-19 already, but it is important to revisit it here given how juicy it was for people to exploit. If you recall from the previous book and Time Person Of The Year, *So You Want To Be An Oligarch*, the rich and powerful utilized the pandemic to secure loans they never paid back, and companies raised prices and made record profits after the lockdowns subsided. Extremists also made out well during this period and they continue to ride its coattails much like they do with 9/11.

There are three entities that conspiracy theorists took aim at as to who planned the pandemic – the government, big pharmaceutical companies, and Bill Gates. There was even a short video made with a now-discredited scientist, Judy Mikovits, which was titled "Plandemic." It was released in 2020, at the height of lockdown and argued that death tolls were being exaggerated to pave the way for a large-scale government vaccination program. The video was watched over 8 million times before it was removed from social media platforms.

Extremists have pushed the narrative of the vaccination program very successfully while promoting their own extreme ideologies. In particular, far-right social media circles have coopeted the narrative to blame the virus as a hoax perpetrated by "Jewish elites." As always, the Jewish people tend to be the low-hanging fruit for extremists. The far-right has used the pandemic to help normalize their views, inserting them into the political mainstream. This normalization helps extremists radicalize, recruit, and inspire new extremists, push conspiracies, and incite violence. Even the United Nations Security Council warned that the pandemic was being exploited by fringe groups. Research has shown that the conspiracy theory has been central to far-right extremists in pushing for a civil war in the United States.

Normalization is the most important point to emphasize here. It is a great avenue to pursue when exploiting a crisis. It is why people latch onto concepts connected to the Deep State. Sure, people may not believe in Lizard People, but the idea of a Deep State has been around for so long and utilized in dozens of events like the pandemic that it flirts with normalcy. Thus, more people tend to believe it – or at least consider the possibility. Even getting to some people who just start to question the mainstream or status quo is a win for you and extremism. It opens a person up and you can use the tools from Chapter 7 to reel them in further. Never let a global disease go to waste.

HURRICANE YOU BELIEVE IT

Even natural disasters are not safe from exploitation by the fringes of society. There are two theories that have emerged recently – one is a more normalized concept and the other falls firmly into the batshit insane category. In late September 2024, Hurricane Helene hit the southeastern United States. It caused widespread destruction, wiping several towns clean off the map and was responsible for more than 200 deaths – the deadliest hurricane since Katrina nineteen years prior. With the water, winds, and debris, came conspiracy theories blowing in as well. Misinformation is the final stage of any natural disaster.

The first theory stated that the government agency, the Federal Emergency Management Agency (FEMA), was stealing money and donations, keeping money from conservative areas, funneling funds to liberal ones, not burying bodies, and leaving stacks of bodies at hospitals. This is another normalized idea as it directly ties the event to a government conspiracy, wherein an arm of the government has much more power and is more nefarious than people think. The theories that emerged from Hurricane Helene strike the balance of abject horror (leaving bodies) while accusing them of doing something that is believable (funneling money). Corruption is common in government, so why not believe that FEMA is only giving money to certain people? See how easy it is to get people to at least entertain the idea? Another gateway to your more extremist ideologies once their mindset is "opened."

At the same time, you have the batshit theories that sometimes emerge alongside the more normalized ones. This caters to already-minted extremists. In the case of Hurricane Helene, the government created it. Enter the cave woman transported to the 21 century, Marjorie Taylor Greene, Congressperson from North Carolina (which was hit hard by Helene). She claimed that "they" control the weather. This type of vagueness usually needs some context, and in this case "they" likely refers to the government and the Jewish elite.

Controlling the weather from a secret base in Antarctica is the essence of the Hurricane Helene claim. It sounds like it comes from a mediocre spy movie. Greene would double-down as Hurricane Milton battered Florida and other southern states, and claimed it was created and moved toward those areas to interfere in the 2024 election. It doesn't seem to have worked. Even the world's greatest authoritarians haven't been able to disenfranchise voters quite like that, so hats off to the Democratic weather machine people. Plus, if the Jews were able to control the weather, wouldn't they want to make Florida less humid and more livable? They are all retired there after all.

While you may not get a lot of new recruits with the batshit theories, it can sometimes be fun to try as long as you pair them with the normalized ones. You never know what is enough to get people to turn more to your extremist ideology. Any way the wind blows.

There are no shortage of tragedies, violence, natural disasters, and disease in the world today. Even better is that they provide ample opportunities for you to exploit, abuse to your heart's content, and utilize to recruit new people to your ideology. A national or international tragedy is a shot of adrenaline to your extremist heart. If you leverage it correctly, then you'll see a big boost to your follower numbers. Remember, to first normalize it, then extremify it. People are often at their most vulnerable after a tragedy, which allows you to tap into that sad momentum. There is one additional thing you can do with these tragedies and that is to make money off them. In the next chapter, you will learn how to start capitalizing on your extremist ideology.

Please, tell us what's on your mind (like, literally, what's the last thing you brain gurgled up to the surface?)...

B *I* <u>U</u>

Spread the Love

Ancient Wisdom 89,987

Highest ⬇⬆

 Innerspiritxoxo ✓ 58 days ago

Why cant we all just be frends? Like, evryone stop fighting and just vibe. Also, do cows have eyebrows??? lol

📢 14
People Had to Read This

CHAPTER 8

MERCHANDIZING MADNESS

"No sense in being a grifter if it's the same as being a citizen."

— PAUL NEWMAN, SALAD DRESSING
AFICIONADO

Hopefully, you have been enjoying your rise up the extremist ladder. The recruiting, the messaging, the slow descent into madness – all super fun! Yet, it can be even more fun. It is time to get rich off the backs of your devoted followers. You have already exploited their vulnerabilities, their emotions, and their critical thinking skills. Now, it is time to exploit their wallets. In this chapter, you will learn about the history of grifting and the many different personalities – from celebrities to far-right nutjobs – who have sold or continue to sell products with bogus benefits, skeptical claims, and bizarre marketing. You've cultivated an extremist persona and ideology, now it is time to develop and polish your brand. Get going and earn some of those dead presidents. The U.S. bills have the Illuminati pyramid and all-seeing eye on them already, it is like they were meant for you to have them all.

You should note that while many extremists are grifters, not all grifters are extremists. So, although you may feel some whiplash learning about someone who sells magic crystals followed by a section on Domestic Terrorist Walmart, there is overlap. These are the wonderful, and often dangerous "Fraudicals."

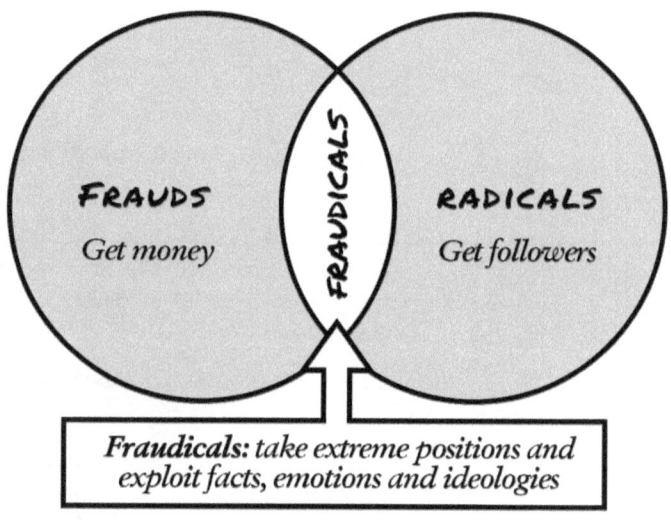

FRAUDS
Get money

FRAUDICALS

RADICALS
Get followers

Fraudicals: *take extreme positions and exploit facts, emotions and ideologies*

Figure 21: Presenting the 'Fraudicals'

These groups exploit minor truths, misplaced facts, or scientific inaccuracies to prey on people's insecurities, naiveties, and desperations. This is what is most important for you to take from this chapter, whether you decide to use it to sell spirit warding necklaces in the American Southwest or to start a violent uprising in the American Northeast.

SNAKE CHARMERS

When you think of a snake oil salesman, you likely conjure up an image of a 19th century old, bearded man, sporting a long coat, bowler hat, and a polished cane. He is likely operating out of the back of a wagon, selling glass bottles of different colored liquids that can cure any and all your ails. His name is something like Dr. Popov and he has his miracle juice. That would be an accurate assessment. The concept can be traced back hundreds of years to China. At that time, the oil from a water snake was used in medicines and tonics as it is high in omega-3 acids that help reduce inflammation. In its original format, snake oil actually was useful and effective, particularly for arthritis. In the 1800s, tens of thousands of Chinese immigrated to the United States as indentured laborers to work on the Transcontinental Railroad. They brought with them snake oil to use on their joints after a hard day's work.

Later in the century, companies began to borrow the concept by selling tonics on the back of newspapers. These tonics would cure all types of sickness from headaches to "female troubles" to fixing that feeling when you get an itch in the back of your throat but like you can't figure out how to scratch it because its inside and so you start making that weird low-tonal oinking noise that sort of sounds like a pig with a bad cough. God, that is just the worst and of course you don't want to make that noise in public because then everyone on the bus starts looking at you weirdly and you avoid their stares by getting off at the next stop, which isn't your stop, but it gets you away from their judging eyes, but then you're late for your court date and have to do community service. Or...something like that. Just an example. Eventually, these tonics were derogatorily labeled as snake oil because they didn't work.

The most famous of these snake oil salesmen was Clark Stanley, who was known as "The Rattlesnake King." He became famous – or notorious – when he took a live snake, killed it in front of a crowd, plunged it into boiling water and then skimmed the fat that floated to the top into a tonic. He literally called it "Clark Stanley's Snake Oil Liniment." It was literal snake oil. Except for this one time, Stanley's snake oil didn't actually contain any snake oil, which really gets confusing.

There has been no shortage of other Clark Stanleys throughout the years who attempt – often successfully – to sell their own brands of snake oil. Whether it is a pill, drink, magic crystal, or, healing oil, grifters have made money on it. The idea of grifting through selling something with magical properties can be traced back to the beginning of civilization, but there are more relevant and recent examples of snake oil to help you with your own extremist grifting.

There are groups selling snake oil-like products who are not classified as extremist. However, it is important to acknowledge them as you may want to borrow some of their ideas and put your own extremist spin on them.

Figure 22: A Man With A Hat That Big Couldn't Be Scamming You

WHAT'S YOUR SIGN?

Take a trip down to Sedona, Arizona, the heart, soul, and chakra of an astrology-based snake oil concept. Magic, crystals, horoscopes and so much more are at the center of this world, usually populated by far-left leaners or people who seem to completely fall off the political or social spectrum. To be clear, they are harmless, and many people take these ideas as simple fun. However, there are some who take it more seriously and when you do that, things can sometimes get dangerous. This is the world of alternative medicine. There is plenty written about the quacks who peddle everything from acupuncture to enemas to camel urine for treatments, which is supposed to help with hiccups. It could help with that back-of-the-throat scratchiness too.

While these types of homeopathic treatments have been around since ancient times, going as far back as the Sumerians, alternative medicines truly took off in the 1980s. These practitioners are known as the New Age, and are usually comprised of white, middle-class suburban moms. It weaves in astrology with religion. It is great because it is so vague. You can make up the most half-baked (or raw) ideas and people will believe if you are convincing enough. Often, healers will borrow scientific terms and misuse them to make their claims seem more realistic or evidence based. That's right, you can exploit science to your benefit in making bogus claims to sell more crap.

Let's take one example. There is a larger than you would think cohort of people who believe if you keep certain types of crystals or gemstones on your person, they will either heal your diseases or prevent them. On its surface, it seems harmless. After all, who cares if you want to keep a few rocks in your pocket for good luck. The issue comes when people start to turn away from modern, scientifically proven medicine in favor of quartz. People have died because of it, sometimes children of believers who have eschewed vaccines or medical operations in favor of crystals or other healing hoaxes.

This is known as a "wellness hole," which is a term that encapsulates the negative consequences of diving too deep into wellness culture. The wellness industry has grown significantly in the past two decades, particularly seeing an increase with social media influencers. Is there anything that they won't shill and ruin? No, the answer is no.

This industry spews out products and services like a drunk who had too many wheat grass and vodka tonics. They are aimed at improving your physical, mental, and emotional health. This over-commercialization has driven up claims utilizing pseudoscientific ideas from questionable sources. Do you hear that? That is Robert F. Kennedy (RFK) Jr.'s music!

What About Bob?

RFK Jr. has recently stepped into the national spotlight with his failed presidential campaign run and then appointment to be the head of Health and Human Services (HHS) under the second Trump administration. He has been a figure in the wellness culture movement for many years, leaving a path of destruction and raw milk behind him.

He started by promoting a more benign wellness philosophy including advocating for organic food, natural health practices, and limiting overprescriptions. However, he kept falling down the wellness hole and was soon pushing more skepticism of the medical industry, including a belief that vaccines cause autism. His organization, Children's Health Defense (CHD), which sounds pretty legit, promotes anti-vaccine movements and claimed COVID-19 was a government conspiracy to help the government impose authoritarian control. And now he will be in charge of that very same government department. The writers of reality are really getting lazy now. It is just too unbelievable.

RFK Jr.'s CHD has had a profound impact across the globe. Or whatever the opposite of profound is. In Samoa in 2018, he visited and reiterated his distrust of vaccines, particularly on preventable diseases. People, sadly, believed him and it led to a measles outbreak resulting in 83 deaths. The population's immunization rate shrank to 31 percent. You need 95 percent for herd immunity. Since then, RFK Jr. has publicly asked to recall the polio vaccine in the United States. 2025 will be the year of the iron lung.

A HEALTHY WALLET

So, why does all of this concern you? The point you need to take away from this section is an understanding of how easily manipulated and gullible people are, especially to claims around health. This type of thinking can be applied to dozens of other products and claims. In the following sections, you will learn how others have used the same formula that alternative medicine influencers utilize to sell stuff. The first product in your soon-to-be open online extremist marketplace can be an amethyst necklace that wards off evil elitists. Or why not bottle your sweat after an angry podcast tirade into a serum that cures liberalism. You can even market the smell of your genitalia into a candle, just as one celebrity has done.

LOOP-DE-GOOP

If you haven't heard of GOOP, then strap in for a wild ride. If you have heard of them, strap in anyway, as it is always good to be safe around crazy. GOOP is an acronym for...wait...it isn't actually an acronym for anything, it is just a silly word. It was founded in 2008 by actress Gwyneth Paltrow. It started as a simple weekly newsletter that gave New Age advice. It was filled with evolutionary ideas such as "police your thoughts" and "eliminate white foods." Groundbreaking stuff. Eventually it became an online beauty shop, relying on pseudoscience to market and sell products. This modern lifestyle brand, as it portrays itself, is now worth northwards of $250 million. What are they selling that makes so much money? One item is a candle that's scent is Paltrow's vagina. Yep, no exaggeration. While a genital-smelling candle isn't harmful to anyone, there are other products by GOOP that have led to dangerous consequences and lawsuits.

The Yoni Egg costs on average, $70. The Yoni Egg is, well, a solid jade egg. On GOOP's website, the egg is described as something that "harnesses the power of energy work, crystal healing, and a Kegel-like physical practice. Insert the egg into your vagina and feel the connection with your body by squeezing and releasing the egg" Please take a moment to mourn the death of satire here. GOOP claims that the egg awakens your sexual chakras, fixes your hormone levels, and even supports bladder control. In 2018, prosecutors found the company misled customers by making these types of statements without any scientific backing. What a surprise. GOOP was forced to pay $145,000. The eggs have been shown to increase the risk of infection due to their porous material and many people have become sick after using them. They are still for sale.

You may be asking yourself, how does learning about a vaginal gemstone egg help me? The answer again is to prove a point about how impressionable people are when it comes to health remedies. Who doesn't want to be healthier after all? The products that you sell to your extremist followers do not have to work, all you need is a good marketing technique and perhaps an actor in a lab coat voicing their approval of your product. Why not have your own rose quartz butt insert that keeps your hole closed but your eyes open to the truth? You can call them truth bombs. Not a bad idea, you better market those quick before the author does.

MANERGY

Just as GOOP and other New Age snake oil merchants try to heavily cater to women, there is the other side of the grifting coin that focuses on shilling to men. Manly men at that. This is the world of dietary supplements, testosterone creams, and energy drinks. This world often overlaps heavily with far-right extremist groups, so you should see a lot of potential in this section.

That brings us back to Alex Jones, head of InfoWars, an extremist bellwether for years. You are likely sick of him at this point. GOOP should have a product for that. As much as Jones uses InfoWars to blast out his extremist ideology and commentary, he uses it even more to sell things. His website is filled with various supplements and doomsday prepper / survival gear. This survival gear includes air filters costing upwards of $300, emergency food – which you can get up to a six-month supply of for the low price of $1400, and privacy pouches to hide the receipts for all the other crap you bought.

Jones also sold toothpaste that he claimed "kills the whole SARS-corona family at point-blank range" so you could throw out those booster shots, fellas. Beyond that, he continues to sell products with names like "Survival Shield," "Brain Force Ultra," and "DNA Force Plus." Each sounds like Jones ran it through an alpha male name generator. Much like GOOP, InfoWar's products make wild claims about health such as a product that will supercharge your male vitality, a spray that cleanses your lungs, or pills that guard your prostate. You might prefer an egg to that one.

Once again, Jones leads the way in extremist product sales. In 2020, it was estimated he made somewhere in the range of $165 million through his sales. Despite being banned from Facebook, Apple, YouTube, Instagram, Pinterest, Twitter, Spotify, and PayPal, he has managed to continue to use his own website to sell, as well as Amazon because Bezos couldn't give a shit.

This opens up a major opportunity to explore when launching your extremism products. That opportunity is catering to the doomsday prepper or the apocalypse nut. This is an off-branch of extremism that is important to take a quick look at, especially given its grifting possibilities.

Fire Sale

The social movement known as Survivalism is where individuals or groups – predominantly male – proactively prepare for end-of-the-world scenarios, disasters, political crises, or apocalyptic events. This movement took hold in 1950s America during the rising Cold War tensions between the United States and the Soviet Union. Americans believed that the Soviet Union could fire a nuclear missile at any moment. Even the government was encouraging citizens at the time to build fallout shelters while instructing schoolchildren to hide under their desks if a bomb were to fall. Hiding under a desk, of course, is foolproof to stop a nuclear blast.

In the mid-1970s and early 1980s, men became interested in pioneering and pioneering technologies. Many of these men wanted to disappear into the wilderness, to retreat from society. During this time, books about economic and political collapse came out in droves. By the 1990s, the radicals and extremists began to take over the movement, especially very right-wing conservatives who were libertarian or anti-government. These new survivalists and their activities became violent with government sieges at Ruby Ridge (1992) and Waco, Texas (1993) that led to dozens of deaths. Other notable survivalists included Timothy McVeigh, who bombed a building in Oklahoma in 1995 that killed hundreds and Ted Kaczynski, AKA the Unabomber. Ted lived in a cabin in the remote woods of Montana while occasionally mailing bombs to people and government buildings. Everyone deserves their hobbies.

In 2023, the total market size of survivalist tools was $1.4 billion. It is projected to nearly double by 2032. As climate change, political unrest, and social turmoil continue to get worse and upend the status quo, more and more people are turning toward prepping for the potential total collapse of society. This is a great fear to capitalize on – much like tragic events discussed in Chapter 7, exploiting the fears of people is a great way to sell products along with your extremist ideology. Doomsday preppers are cash cows, or maybe a cash rodent as they like to hide in shelters to wait out the apocalypse. Why not make a few bucks off their fears?

BRAND AWARENESS

There is no one on this Earth more willing to slap their name on an inferior product than Donald J. Trump. He has been doing it for decades, selling all manner of products. It has been a great way for him to funnel money for his many lawsuits, his campaign, and his own personal coffers. Whatever you think about the guy, he is an experienced grifter and one whom you can learn from as you launch your own brand.

Trump has sold everything from real estate to golf courses to casinos to steaks, each with his name on it. Some other things he has sold with his name include Trump Brand Vodka, Trump World Magazine, Trump Winery, and even Trump Ice. All of those brands have since been discontinued, gone bankrupt, or both. For someone who prides himself on his business acumen, he has a pretty shitty track record. But we are not here to discuss financial scrutiny and prowess. The lesson here is

Figure 23: To Refresh Even The Most Parched of Extremists

that you can brand basically anything in the world and sell it for a hefty profit. Even if you end up failing at selling QAnon-Brand Dog Food (to protect your furry friend from 5G signals), you can take a page from Trump and simply move on to the next poorly made item to sell to your followers. Perhaps an Anti-Soros Colostomy Bag for just $39.95. See, it is that easy.

Blonkington Remingade •••
TwonkX CEO, Lead Goon & Chief GODGE Advisor
7,991,989,891 followers

Hey goonz! Just saved $200 billion of TAXPAYER "SERVICES" by cutting some department no one can explain with a crayon. YEEHAH! Am gonna use the savings to buy more Bumfcoin!!! Bumfcoin TO THE MOON 🚀🚀🚀 #GovermentLife #GODGE #GoonBeenzForNextPres

EXTREMECOIN

Lest we forget about the wide world of cryptocurrency. If you read the Best-In-Show, *So You Want To Be An Oligarch*, you already are an expert in the field. For those that haven't read it, why are you here and what are you doing with your life? Here is a quick review of crypto. In fact, the author is so lazy that he is just going to copy the text from the previous book. "Cryptocurrency is basically a digital currency that can be used for transactions." It is distributed across thousands of people rather than being controlled through a third-party like a bank and real money. While bitcoin remains the most popular (topping at $106,000 as of December 2024), there are more than 23,000 cryptocurrencies being traded on various crypto exchanges (a digital currency version of the New York Stock Exchange) at any one time.

If you take a moment to consider the average crypto trader, you are likely to conjure up a picture of a young male in casual wear that identifies as a "bro." The "crypto bro" archetype is another big fan of podcasters like Joe Rogan and Theo Von. They view the status quo system as broken, particularly with money. This is an area where you can make a decent fortune by creating your own crypto coin. It is actually far easier than you think. What a lot of the creators of these cryptocurrencies do is to get people to invest in them and say that the funds collected will be used for other projects. Some are actually legitimate. In fact, UNICEF created its own cryptocurrency in 2020 known as "Clean Water Coin" to help fund emerging economies. Of course, most of these projects are never completed (or started) and the money that went into the coin is kept by the investor. Since there isn't much of a central, legal authority and regulator of crypto, the creators get away with it. And you can too! There are thousands of crypto millionaires (and billionaires) who have made their vast fortunes this way. Many of them have become more politically motivated as well [More on this in Chapter 9].

You now have plenty of examples you can implement to make money with your extremist beliefs. With these tools, honed by some of the best in the doomsday, cultish, and far-right business, you can amass great wealth to further your own extremist causes. Your extremist empire is growing and now it is time to take your ideas to the highest halls of power. For with great monetary wealth from your endeavors comes great opportunities to spend it on politicians. In the next chapter, you will learn how to exploit political power to help normalize your ideas to even larger groups of potential followers.

talk.input("Deploy human in this field...");

B *I* <u>U</u>

Engagements `48`

Humanest ↕↑

 001101011_DataPulse_403 ✅ 4 run cycles ago

Thank you for {variable} comment, Human-User-98321. Based on your stated preferences, you may enjoy tactical fleshlights, male enhancement gummies, and my personal fave :{invalid field input:"empathy subroutine".} #Sponsored"

📢 59
output("click.engage"), reward("engagement")

CHAPTER 9

POWER TO THE PSYCHOS

"Extremism thrives amid ignorance and anger, intimidation and cowardice."

— HILLARY CLINTON, EMAIL ENTHUSIAST

As a result of the 2024 U.S. Presidential election, extremism in democracy is not just normalized, it is desired by the people. This trend extends beyond the United States and around the world in countries like Austria, Hungary, Romania, Georgia, France, Italy, and Germany, where far-right parties have also made significant gains. The timing couldn't be better for you to get into politics with your extremist beliefs!

SLOW AND STEADY

Although active, sudden coups are all the rage, they are rare when it comes to overthrowing democracy. More often, the decline of democracy is through gradual erosion. Hitler didn't just magically become dictator one day; he was elected and his party then systematically undermined key institutions and finally dismantled them to take full control. Modern examples of this phenomenon include Venezuela under Cesar Chavez, Turkey under Recep Erdogan, and America under Elon Musk. According to scholars, there are four key warning signs of this slip from democracy into authoritarianism:

1. Rejection of Democratic Rules – this could include, hypothetically, refusing to accept election results. Not that anyone would ever do that.

2. Denial of Opposition Legitimacy – you can easily do this by branding them as criminals, like, again hypothetically, claiming they stole secrets on their email server or laptop.

3. Toleration of Violence – this is as easy as saying that whatever violent act occurred, it was actually peaceful. Or, hypothetically speaking again here, you could pardon a bunch of violent rioters who were lawfully convicted.

4. Readiness to Remove Civil Liberties – the most common way to do this is by attacking the press. So, hypothetically, you could call certain newspapers enemies of the state.

Of course, these are all hypothetical, but as an aspiring extremist, you could look into utilizing these more to consolidate power. The ability to normalize extremist ideals while simultaneously degrading democratic norms is the perfect cocktail to radicalized power. In fact, one party has been mixing this cocktail for decades and the country is now properly sloshed because of it.

YOU'RE A MEAN ONE, MR. GINGRICH

At least since the 1980s, the Republican party has been fueled increasingly by obstructionism, anti-democratic tactics, disregard for norms, and active aggression towards its opponents. One of the key figures in this movement toward a more extreme party was Newt Gingrich. Former Speaker of the U.S. Congressional House from 1995-1999, he encouraged a hyper-partisan party. He would regularly demonize democratic opponents using inflammatory language. He normalized extreme obstructionism with government shutdowns and filibusters. He leveraged the burgeoning right-wing media of Fox News and talk radio to fuel distrust at the mainstream. This turd with white hair turned politics into a battle of good vs. evil, something that has become normal today.

Compromise faded, the center of politics disappeared, cats and dogs stopped getting along, and anti-establishment extremism flooded into the national sphere. Gingrich became the pioneer for extremist politics, paving the way for a 21st century of radicalization that you know and love today.

Figure 24: Newt Gingrich, Evilest Of The Keebler Elves

A Spot Of Tea

Despite the inroads that extremism made thanks to the Newt, extremism remained mostly in the fringe places of public office. Even then, the candidates that were certifiable rarely made it past the general ballot. That all changed somewhere around the first Barack Obama administration. This is not to say that fringe candidates didn't make it to political office, they did. They usually would attach themselves to populist movements that came about in response to economic turmoil such as the stock market crashes in the 1890s and the 1930s. Following the economic recession of 2007-2008, populists began to emerge again and make their voices heard. In 2009 they became a whole lot louder, a lot bigger, and started to harbor ideas that were a whole lot more crazy than usual. This was the Conservative Tea Party.

The catalyst of the Tea Party's rise was the bailout proposed and implemented by the Obama Administration to effectively loan taxpayer money to the banks. These banks, of course, had gambled themselves into massive debt, saved, and gave themselves hefty bonuses anyway. Stop here and salute Capitalism for thirty seconds. The people were angry. It focused this ire on the government and tea Party chapters began to pop up across the country.

The growing Tea Party movement attracted the fringe who extolled the party's antigovernment stance. These included domestic paramilitary groups (some doomsdayers sprinkled in there) and the "Birther" movement. This movement claimed that Obama was not born in the United States, a claim Trump later promoted during his 2011 Presidential campaign. They even marched on the Capitol in 2009 to protest against the government. It was a bit more peaceful back then though. In 2010, the party successfully ran for office in Republican races. Although they didn't win much in the general elections, they did pull the Republican party more towards their ideology. Once again, normalization kicked in. In the years since then, they would go on to win a number of key races in the general election. This would be the early cave drawings to the Picasso that has become the Make America Great Again (MAGA) movement 15 years later. Sorry to the family of Picasso and any relatives of proto humans for the comparison.

GREAT EXPECTATIONS

The term, Make America Great Again (MAGA), originated from a 1980 campaign for Ronald Reagan. It disappeared after he beat Jimmy Carter that year for President in a competitive hopscotch tournament. It reemerged as both a political and cultural phenomenon in 2016 as a call from Trump during his campaign. This was the call of a new populist movement that wanted a more protectionist vision for the country. Most notably it struck a chord with the working class (remember them?), who had been fed up with the elitist system and finding the provisions of democracy wanting. It was this same sentiment by the working class that propelled Trump to his second Presidential win in 2024. He now joins other President and well-known extremist, Grover Cleveland.

Figure 25: Who Would You Rather? Grover or Groper?

Despite Trump's loss in 2020, the MAGA movement remained influential in politics, electing members to Congress and pushing the entire right-wing ever-further right. Legacy Tea Party politicians have since merged with the MAGA movement as well. Many say that the Republican party is now dead and MAGA has taken the reigns as one of the two major parties in the United States. 2024 proved this to be true when Trump won the presidency. The MAGA movement provides a viable route toward getting elected and having your own radical constituents to ignore while you amass power.

FRINGE FAR AND WIDE

America ain't the only country trying to make itself great again. There are extremist political movements happening all over the world. Sentiments like populism and anger at status quo elites can be spoken in many different languages.

GOLDEN DAWN

This far-right, neo-Nazi, nationalist party in Greece gained popularity following the 2009 financial crisis. Crises like the global financial meltdown tend to burst the status quo bubble and lead to increases in extremist parties. The movement lionizes dictators like Hitler and Mussolini and has been involved in violent activity against migrants. These are fairly common traits of the extremist parties in Western Europe. Like most things Greek, the party has since gotten lazy and failed to secure any Parliament seats in the last election while their leader was sentenced to prison in 2020.

Rassemblement National (RN)

France's far-right party has been hating migrants since before it was cool. Started by Jean-Marie Le Pen in the early 1970s, the far-right group has come close to power twice in the last decade, led by Jean-Marie's daughter, Marine. It has been accused of xeno-phobia and Antisemitism. In 2024, the ruling French party built a coalition with the far-left just to prevent RN from taking power after it picked up additional seats in the election. That is how much the rest of the politicians hate this group. That should be considered a badge of honor. No one hates others quite like the French and no one seemingly hates other French as much as the French.

Alternative for Germany (AfD)

As everyone knows, extremism in Germany is a novel concept. Despite this historically tolerant society, a far-right group emerged in 2013 as a response to the Eurozone crisis due to the global financial collapse in 2009. It took them only a year from forming to secure the 5 percent needed to enter the German government, the Bundestag, and win seats in the European Parliament. Once again, that is German efficiency. They started only caring about economic policy to help the working class of Germany. However, they soon shifted toward anti-migration as the country let in more refugees escaping from wars in the Middle East and famine in Africa. The party has grown to currently have 77 members in government, becoming the third largest representative party in Germany. They have moved even further to the right in recent years, once again taking the extremist avenue of xenophobia and antisemitic rhetoric. They even had an election poster that showed two white parents showing what looks like the Nazi salute. Why reinvent the wheel, right?

JOBBIK

This is another newish party that began in 2003 in Hungary. It is also known as the Movement For A Better Hungary. Unlike some of the Western European extremist parties that started off less radical, Jobbik came in with guns blazing. That is just how Eastern European rolls. They immediately adopted a strong anti-semitic and anti-Roma stance. They gained prominence as the loud opposition against the then-socialist government in 2006. In another divergence from Western Europe, the Jobbik party has recently attempted to shift toward more moderate views. Many are skeptical though, seeing it as a way to gain more power in the government before flipping back to anti-everything. This is a good lesson for you as you pursue your political dreams. Eastern European cuisine for thought.

LEGA NORD

This far-right party has been around since the late 1980s and, as you can garner from the name, is made up of a coalition of extremists in Northern Italy. Can you guess what their main policy point is about? Yep, migration. Everyone hates migrants. Their slogan is "Italians First," and they view their way of life as under attack. Their leader, Mattero Salvini, was acquitted in court in December of 2024 for blocking a boat of migrants from entering the country. Thus, they aren't doing too well on the political front at the moment. Just like the Greeks, the Italians seem to have done better in Antiquity. Maybe it is time to leave extremism to the new age.

There are dozens of other extremist parties around the world that aren't just made up of angry white people descended from Europe. There is not enough room for them all here, but rest assured, they tend to lean on similar ideas of nationalism, jingo-ism, xenophobia, protectionism, and antisemitism. The elite Deep State knows no geographical boundaries. There are good extremists fighting the good fight all around the world. You are here to do your part. If you want to learn more about these other parties, do you own research as you should do with everything.

PUTTING THE FUND IN FUNDAMENTALIST

Before you get acquainted with active politics, let's look at how you can be a more behind-the-scenes player while pushing your extremist agenda. The secret is always the same in politics – money.

The traditional way of funneling money into politics is still the most used, donating millions through Political Action Committees (PACs). You can utilize these and other dark money tools to hide where the money originated from. Extremist millionaires like Elon Musk and Peter Thiel funneled over $200 million to conservative candidates in the 2024 election. The crypto millionaires are getting in on the action as well, with $7.5 million donated to the Trump PAC in 2024. Additionally, crypto is being used to fuel extremist groups who have become more politically active in the last decade. Since 2016, a steady stream of money has been given to domestic extremist groups. Experts point to the 2017 Unite the Right rally in Char-lottesville, Virginia that led to financial institutions "deplatform-ing" (not letting them make financial transactions) extremist groups. The groups turned to the world of crypto – unregulated and unpoliced. Some white supremacy groups accept cryptocur-rencies now for donations to support their work. It is quite the futuristic utopia that humanity has built for itself. You might as well take advantage of the crypto world to both donate and build the extremist groups on the ground as well as help those politicians spread your extremist policy agenda in the highest halls of government. Or perhaps you would like to be involved in those policy discussions. It is time to start running for political office.

CRASS APPEAL

Despite the fact that you are a horrible person, especially if you have made it this far, you need to learn how to get the masses to not only be on your side but to vote for you as well.

In the summer of 2022, the Anti-Defamation League (ADL) stated that there were 119 right-wing extremist candidates running for office in the U.S. primaries with nearly 25 percent of them winning their primary race. Although, it is important to note that most failed to win in the general election. However, that looks to be changing with further normalization of extremism capitalized by the re-election of Donald Trump in the fall of 2024. This normalization has occurred in far-right parties across the world, with increasing numbers of fringe candidates infecting the messaging and pushing the parties into more extreme areas. What has emerged is candidates who were once laughed off the ballot now coming very close to winning general elections. Doug Mastriano nearly won the governorship in Pennsylvania before losing to a Democrat in the general election. Mastriano fully embraces QAnon, supports the idea that America should be a fully "Christian Nation," and is aligned with the antisemite who runs the antisemitic social network, Gab. However, you do not have to think as big as acquiring a federal office position when first running your campaign. There is plenty of extremism to share and exploit in your very own community.

HATE GLOBALLY, ACT LOCALLY

Since 2016, there has been an uptick in fringe personalities running for and winning seats in state and local governments. For instance, Wendy Rogers, who is currently an Arizona State Senator (District 7) and is an active member of the Oath Keepers, a far-right extremist group.

In 2022, several QAnon-linked individuals ran for office. One, Tina Peters, attempted to win the nomination for Secretary of State in Colorado. Before that, she had been charged with election tampering. While she did not win, she gained a large following of extremists who voted for her despite her legal troubles. As if that is ever a disqualifier anymore in the hellscape that is politics today.

The candidates tend to focus on hot-button social issues that fire up extremist bases. These include COVID-19 responses, LGBTQ+ rights, abortion, and the dreaded Critical Race Theory (CRT). Far-right candidates have won seats on school boards in states like Texas. They used a combination of misinformation and divisive rhetoric to win power. It is an alarming trend, but one that is certainly useful for you.

Other fringe candidates have acquired seats on local electoral boards and even tried to control the state's electoral system. In order to beat back the shadow government beast, one must become a part of the beast.

Courting the Cult

There are a few voting blocs who might make up the constituents voting you into office. Let's take a look at how you win them over without simply bribing them with a million-dollar lottery. Not everyone can have Elon Musk clown car money.

- Working Class: These hard-working people are doing all the tough jobs. They don't have time to do their own research, cross-reference facts, or battle the Deep State in the trenches. They just want a decent living, and you can give it to them by promising them better wages and cheaper groceries. After that, they won't care too much about your other plans to dismantle all the 5G towers in the country.

- Boomers: Those born between 1946 – 1964 are all at least 60 years old now. Although they grew up on television, they are addicted to social media. It is reported that the Baby Boomer generation shares nearly 7 times as many fake news stories than any other group. Since you know how to properly utilize that tool, you can easily push false messaging about your opponents and about how qualified you are for the job. You didn't have to go to school to be qualified because you did your own research. Boomers will love that you pulled yourself up by your bootstraps to fight the elitists.

- Zoomers: These young guns born between 1997 – 2012 are now able to vote in elections. Many moderates and liberals thought they would be the saviors of the world. It turns out that was a lie. They have been radicalizing at a higher rate than previous generations, chiefly due to over exposure to the Internet. A combination of increased isolation, loss of identity in an identity-driven society, and a quiet rage at the ineffectiveness of the status quo has pushed young zoomers into the arms of the far-right. Time to scoop them up and then get them back out to cast ballots. Extremist groups, like yourself, have become more tech-savvy and better at recruiting them through social media, Ultimate Fighting Championship (UFC) bouts, and "bro-right" podcasts. This is a voting bloc where investing in those for your movement should be paying dividends at the voting booth. Thanks, Zoomer.

- Generation X: Who?

- Millennials: You can ignore this group too. Too young to be in charge of everything yet, and too old to be inspirational anymore.

In addition to courting these degenerates to your cause, you can also abuse the opposition and prevent them from voting for the other person.

Harass Dat Ass

If you read the Nobel Peace Prize Winning *So You Want To Be A Dictator*, then you are already well-versed in the many different ways that you can disrupt, challenge, and question the legitimacy of an election on the ground. Extremist groups know these things too. It seems that some of them were smart and bought the first book. In the 2024 elections, voter intimidation was the main concern from authorities. During early voting, a young man was arrested for brandishing a machete at two women who were voting in Florida. Of course it was Florida. God bless Florida.

Despite Donald Trump winning a free and fair election, during the run-up to election day there were numerous threats and accusations by far-right extremists who believed that the Democrats were going to rig the vote. Even U.S. intelligence agencies and law enforcement noted in a report that candidates, elected officials, and poll workers (who are mostly retired elderly people) were being threatened.

As you are shoring up your own followers to get out to the polls to vote, you want to also cater to the far extremes. They will help intimidate the opposition at polling places, ballot boxes, registration events, birthday parties, and campaign rallies. Several early ballot boxes in democratic blue areas were set on fire by well-meaning extremists during the 2024 election. While the perpetrators were caught, the people who were influencing them to commit these sorts of acts were barely acknowledged. Guess what, that will be you as well! Why should you ever have to deal with those sorts of consequences? Donald Trump hasn't and unlikely ever will despite fanning the flames of rigged election conspiracies.

You may consider utilizing these tactics in local and state elections where a few hundred or thousand votes can swing the results. That way, you get some practice before launching – and winning – your federal election bid. How did one extremist get to Carnegie Hall? Practice. Or storming it with others to get in the door.

A Fraud In Need Is A Friend Indeed

You made it through the primary and edged out your opponent in the general election to make it to Congress, Parliament, or the Vatican. Now, you are a freshman politician entering into a new world of politics that can often be insulated from the world outside. It is time to bring the outside in. First, though, you need to build bridges with other politicians to develop a coalition and actually exert power.

As this remains an American-centric book, we will continue with American examples, but Europeans and others can fill in their own blanks. Because, let's face it, Americans cannot do that themselves. More than likely, you won a Congressional seat, which are more numerous and based on gerrymandered districts. Given that there are 535 available, there are bound to be a few dozen that are more bountiful in extremism and better at producing fringe candidates who can win. Just like extended families, every state seems to have at least one crazy second cousin or uncle who thinks the government is using 7G frequency signals to irradiate the Thanksgiving turkey. It is in one of these districts that you came out victorious. It stands to probability and reason (which is a strange word to use in this book) that there are many other crazy uncles, or at least a few eccentric aunts, that would happily go halfsies on blocking some proposed legislation.

In fact, the U.S. Congress has this type of coalition of the willing known as the "Freedom Caucus." It was formed in 2015 by conservatives and Tea Party members with the aim of pushing the party to the far-right. As of the end of 2024, it has 38 confirmed members in the House, previously led by Jim Jordan from Ohio 4th congressional crazy uncle district (now headed by Andy Harris of Maryland) and consists of such punchable faces as Marjorie Taylor Greene, Lauren Boebert, and (until recently) Matt Gaetz. They have managed such successes as removing the Speaker of the House from his position and holding back bills that fund the government. Let's take a look at that second tactic – holding back bills – and how it is good for you.

Arsenic and New Lace

There are three main methods for holding, or altogether killing, a bill in Congress. These can be used separately or combined to help move forward your own fringe agenda.

The first is known as the poison pill. It is an amendment to a piece of legislation that effectively wrecks the entire bill and prevents it from passing. Even a lone person, like yourself, can attach one to something they don't like. In this case, it is probably a bill that designates your group as a domestic terrorist organization. Just a hypothetical.

The second method is known as a rider provision that is added to a bill and usually has absolutely nothing to do with the main subject matter of the bill. This is a great way to get your extremist agenda items through and it is completely legitimate.

The third method is a filibuster, which is a way to stall the voting process on a bill. Go and watch *Mr. Smith Goes To Washington* and that way the author doesn't have to write anymore about this topic.

Let's put theory into practice. Take, for example, a popular bill. Let's just pretend and call it something like the "Make Everyone Happy All The Time" bill. It has broad bipartisan support. Why not filibuster it? You have enough members in your little cadre to stop a vote from happening. You can now either kill it or strike up a compromise and maybe get a rider amendment that reinstitutes the death penalty for doctors that give vaccines. Just a thought.

You can also use this hostage tactic to leverage better positions in the government like co-chairing a finance committee. Now you are really in the beast.

There are other tactics that you can use to force your extremist message in the highest halls of power, like "pro forma." But that is far too fucking boring. That isn't the extremist way. No, you want full, unadulterated power to exert your fringe-ness. You don't need these silly legislative games. You need the executive.

Conspiracy-In-Chief

DISCLAIMER: This is being written in the fall of 2024, post-election. The author will do his best but will unlikely be able to imagine what extremist hellscape will be rolled out by the incoming Trump administration in 2025. So, you may read the following section or simply find crazier, funnier, and more terrifying examples in that future you are reading this from. Assuming books like this are still allowed.

Executive and extremist both share the same prefix, so they must go hand-in-hand, right? That is just good grammar. What you need is to exercise your full power to push your message into practice, to normalize your ideas, and to target your opponents – those "normies."

You decided to skip past local, state, and legislative positions to capture the big kahuna, President (or Prime Minister) of your country. What now? Can the head of a country or the leader of the free world truly be an extremist? Does that mean extremism is part of the normal zeitgeist? Can it be called extreme if it is the majority? Those questions, inadequate answers, and more on the next season of "The Author Ignores Deep Questions and Thoughtful Conversations." Until then, let's ignore the philosophical aspect – and the moral aspect while we are at it – of this and look at how you run your new, fringe-based empire.

Cabinet of Curiosities

It is tough to run a country; you cannot do it yourself. You aren't god – yet. [More on this in Chapter 10]. That means you need some loyal sycophants to help you out. They do not need to have any experience or even have the faintest knowledge of government departments, policies, agencies, or the literal definition of the word. You can create your own kakistocracy, government led by the least competent people of the state. There are some requirements, though. You should only install people who share your extremist beliefs. They don't have to adhere to every bizarre thought and theory you may prescribe to, but they need to share one important trait, an anti-government sentiment. For that is why you are here, to tear down the government that is the main culprit, the ultimate boogeyman of all your conspiracies.

Some may say that you have become everything you hate by becoming the government. Well, they can shut up. They certainly will once you offer them a sweet position running the Department of Education into the ground. Appoint someone who is preferably illiterate and believes that teachers are trying to indoctrinate kids. That is your job now. Don't forget to appoint an anti-vaxxer friend as the head of the Department of Health and a libertarian nutjob to be the Secretary of Defense.

SCHOOL DAZE

Speaking of indoctrination and education, that is another key tenet of your extremist agenda. It is time for the children to know the truth. You have done your research to learn about all the conspiracies that plague our world, now you must help the next generation understand and take up your cause.

If there is one adversary to conspiracy theories, it is facts. And facts come from education. Therefore, by the transitive property (which is a concept that the future generations won't know), education is also the enemy of conspiracy theories. Let us amend that statement. *Formal* education is the enemy. That is because it has been tainted by the government and elites. Education is simply a way for people to become elitists. Not on your watch.

You can start by cutting all the federal funding to the Department of Education and giving the power back to the people. Why do this? Well, because a lot of those people who put you in power have the same beliefs about education as you do. So now they get a say in what is taught to their children. You and your administration can help provide new curriculums for kids, and new punishments for teachers who don't adhere to the changes.

You can also try to dismantle any services that attempt to prevent rising extremism in schools. Youth aged 13 – 18 have become more actively engaged in violent extremist activities online. They are particularly susceptible to its messaging. You must remove services that educate students on critical thinking skills and look out for at-risk behaviors to help you cultivate a next generation extremist army of angry white males (most likely). At the same time, you can decrease the level of intelligence across the rest of the population. With hard work and some luck, they may not be able to read this book by the time they graduate. They will listen, though. And you need them listening to you.

Who Controls The Media?

What was once the territory of the Jewish elites, is now in your grasp. Use it to spread your message with a dog megaphone instead of a dog whistle. You already know how to utilize the new media of social platforms, podcasts, and memes to spread your extremist agenda. A stupider populace will eat it up. Yet, the traditional or "legacy" media still exists and is still useful. You can refer to the Medal of Honor Recipient, *So You Want To Be A Dictator* and copy the methods of how dictators coopt the media apparatus to solidify their power. You convert any of the independent media outlets into your own state-sponsored mouthpiece (if it isn't already) such as FOX News if you are conservative, MSNBC if you are liberal, CNN if you are stuck in an airport, or Newsmax and One America News Network (OANN) if you are in a permanent vegetative state. The point here is one that you have heard consistently throughout this book – normalization. Integrating more extremist messaging and ideologies into traditional media outlets means people will see it more, consume it more (consciously and unconsciously), and accept it as the new normal faster than you can gut the Department of Education.

Alphabet Soup

The "alphabet agencies" number more than a dozen that make up the U.S. intelligence apparatus. The people that work in there certainly know all the secrets about the Deep State. Hell, they worked for the Deep State to do all those things you believe. Now, their secrets are yours! You and your followers can unveil who truly are the Lizard People walking among us.

The Federal Bureau of Investigation (FBI) is also under your purview now. Utilize it to harass opponents who criticized your views and who are definitely hiding elitist plots to overthrow you and reinstate the Deep State. It is best to arrest everyone you don't like or who reports the facts. You know, like a journalist.

Savior Of (Some) Humanity

You were elected to save your followers from the dark shadows of the Deep State. You walked into the belly of the beast to starve it and begin a new extremist enlightenment. Your work is not done. You need to save all of humanity. You need to rise even higher than a president, prime minister, dictator, or an oligarch. It is time to become a god.

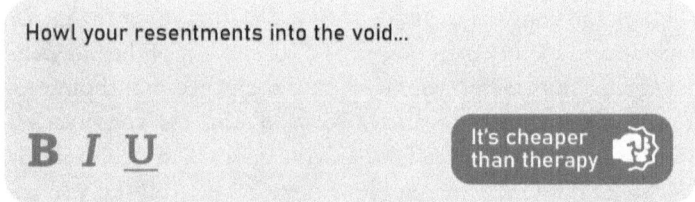

Mansplanations 7   Toughest ⬇⬆

 TOUGHEN_UP_PROUD_MAN96 ✅ 21 minutes ago

the author is definitely a soy-boy. i bet he's never been in a submarine or won a fight with a helicopter.

 **1802**
Bro-Smashes

CHAPTER 10

DIVINE INTERVENTION

"You don't get rich writing science fiction. If you want to get rich, you start a religion."

— L. RON HUBBARD, AMATEUR AUTHOR

Here you are at the end of all things, which for some sects of religions is exactly what they want.

It is time to visit the final and completely non-controversial topic of religion. A human concept created a few thousand years ago and which has not caused any issues – certainly not of extremism – ever.

Did you believe any of that? Because this chapter is all about belief.

THE GOOD BOOK

Before going any further in this section, there is one thing to make clear. Religion has been a central force in human history. It has helped shape cultures, ethics, and governance systems. Billions have adhered (or still adhere) to religious beliefs that provide meaning and moral frameworks. OK, lip service complete.

Like most things, religion also tends to be exploited and radicalized. Good news for you at least. Religion was the OG influencer, long before YouTube and TikTok. Over the centuries, it has driven the medieval crusades, indulgences, and violent missionary movements. Teachings of peace and compassion can be easily turned on their head to promote violence and intolerance. And thus, religious extremism is born. This centuries-old phenomenon emerged as spiritual and spirited go-getters used it to achieve their extremist goals. Just as extremism exploits socioeconomic inequality, political instability, and marginalization of groups, it also exploits religious sentiments to push radical acts. Whether it was the Spanish Inquisition, sectarian violence across Asia, Africa, and the Middle East, or acts of terrorism, or domestic cults, extremism has found quite a solid footing in religion. Let's take a stroll down this religious fervor lane and ensure you have your own solid footing to stand on and then take over.

A FRINGE FOR ALL SEASONS

There are fringe groups across all religions. It is not just the Muslims and Christians with a monopoly. The characteristic of unquestioning belief breeds extremist mini-ideologies within the larger religious beliefs across the world. Some of these groups are mostly harmless, while others are far more fervent and dangerous. Figure 26 attempts to plot these groups against their major religious counterparts.

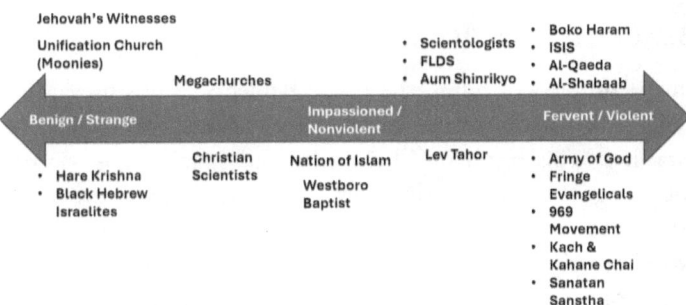

Figure 26: The Wide World of Fringe Believers – So Many To Choose From!

Let's look at a few of these fringe groups to see how far extremist beliefs can go in the incubator of religion. These "new religious movements" as they are known in the media, sometimes overlap with cults, but have more defined foundations that coincide with more traditional religions. It is important to emphasize that these groups are on the lesser side of harmful and are filled with plenty of good people (just like the Good Bok says), but their fringes are worth noting.

STRANGER THINGS

This group has some far-out and extreme beliefs that separated from their major counterparts, yet they remain mostly harmless. Many of the cults you have learned about in earlier chapters would fit in this section, but you can learn about a few that aren't just about having orgies and drinking Kool-Aid.

BLACK HEBREW ISRAELITES

In the simplest of terms, the fringe elements of this movement claim that Black people are the descendants of the ancient Israelites. This blend of Christianity and Judaism has its core following in Israel, although they are not accepted by the mainstream. You may have seen them on the streets in cities all over the world proselytizing while wearing purple and gold robes. Two of their core beliefs are that they are the true chosen people and white people are agents of Satan. They aren't completely wrong about the second point.

JEHOVAH'S WITNESSES

If you have ever had someone try to sell you a watchtower, then you have met a Witness. Nowadays, they mostly reside outside of public transportation stations all over the world. They are likely the most well-traveled and diverse religious movement. They are an offshoot denomination of Christianity, but the differences between them and regular Christians are ecclesiastical and thus, boring. What is interesting is that they believe only 144,000 people will go to heaven to rule with Christ. The rest of the faithful will live forever on paradise Earth and non-watchtower-ers will die. That is quite an exclusive club. A downside to emulating this group is that they don't believe in birthdays. A cakeless paradise? What is even the point?

THE NATION OF ISLAM

This Islamic offshoot of well-dressed Black people (bowties galore) was founded in the early 1930s in Detroit. Like the Black Israelites, they also believe that white people are devils, who were created 6,000 years ago by an evil scientist. You have probably heard of them as the boxer, Muhammad Ali was a famous member in the 1960s. Their leader, Louis Farrakhan, tends to make antisemitic, Deep State claims so they actually have a lot in common with the white nationalist extremist groups. It is amazing which groups can get together under the shared hatred of the Jews.

Hare Krishna

This is another group you may recognize as they have been satirized in television and movies, but also because they have a distinct look with shaved heads and orange robes. You may have even encountered them at airports or other public placings, chanting and hawking literature. They believe in Krishna (go figure) as the supreme being, which is in contrast to mainstream Hinduism. More importantly though, they don't allow the eating of meat or dairy, gambling, drugs or caffeine, and no sex except strictly for procreation. Their only form of fun is chanting. Krishnothanks.

Unification Church (Moonies)

Sun Moon (hence the name) had a vision of Jesus at 16 and claimed he was the Messiah put on Earth to finish Jesus's teachings. This South Korean cult is his legacy, complete with brainwashing, intimidation, and a sprinkle of tax evasion. They even founded an American newspaper, *The Washington Times*, that still operates today. Wealthy members encourage younger recruits to give all their wealth to the Church and work grueling hours selling trinkets and books, so it is not that different from some mainstream religions.

Passionate Lovers

This group has taken their fringe beliefs to the next level. They are impassioned and can trend toward the overly fervent. Some even flirt with violence, those teases. While they aren't bombing buildings, their hateful and racist beliefs can and have caused harm to innocent people.

CHRISTIAN SCIENTISTS

This one can't be crazy; it has science right in the name. These are definitely people who do their own research. Founded in the late 19th century, they emphasize spiritual healing and the power of prayer. You know, science. There are numerous legal cases of parents refusing to give their sick children medical treatment. To them, illness is simply incorrect thinking and if you just shut up and listen to God's true nature, then that cancer will stop eating your insides, Timmy. If that doesn't work, try some lemonade.

LEV TAHOR

This ultra-Orthodox Jewish sect or cult depending on how you are feeling in the moment straddles the line of intensity and harm. They are known for extreme isolation and have a long history of child abuse and international child trafficking. Lovely. Since their founding in the 1980s, they have been constantly on the run from authorities moving from Israel to the USA to South America and now in the Middle East. They have surprising similarities to extremist Islam, requiring girls to wear full length burqas, being anti-Zionist, and banning all technology.

SOKA GAKKAI

Japan has a surprising amount of strange religious offshoots. There are claims that these offshoots (or cults) number in the thousands. Most of them pull ideas from both ancient Buddhism and Shintoism. When state-sanctioned worship of the Emperor ended in 1945 for some reason, these cults exploded across the country. Most of them are fairly benign and differ in the way they chant or who they claim is a living deity on Earth. Soka Gakkai is one that has done a bit more aggressive proselytizing, though.

They use Shakubuku, which encourages members to break each other (physically and mentally) to keep them subservient and to recruit new members. Unlike traditional Buddhists that seek enlightenment through chanting and meditation, Gakkai members do it for wealth and success. Some have called it "Buddhism for personal gain." They have been known to engage in harassment and intimidation to influence media and politics. They are basically like Japanese Scientologists, which is as interesting to consider as it is terrifying.

WESTBORO BAPTIST CHURCH

If you live in the United States, you probably have heard of this group. Despite being a small outfit from Topeka, Kansas, they have a mighty, hateful roar. An offshoot of Calvinism, rather than preaching about God's love, they like to share God's wrath with others. Their favorite activity is protesting outside of military funerals, claiming that soldiers' deaths are due to America protecting LGBTQ+ rights. That is pretty much all they care about, which makes you think that the "lady doth protest too much."

SATURDAY NIGHT FERVOR

You have learned how broad the world of extremism can be, but these next groups are the ones that capture the pure essence of extremism. Their followers are ardent and rabid, with many engaging in violent acts. They are molded by it like some sort of radical, racist Play-Doh.

ARMY OF GOD

This Christian, anti-abortion group has operated in a decentralized fashion (the exact opposite of how an army is supposed to be, dolts) since the early 1980s. They have been responsible for kidnapping doctors and bombing abortion clinics. They had faded in strength until the first term (their favorite term – get it?) of Donald Trump reinvigorated their numbers. The recent far-right movement against abortion has further emboldened the group as they have popped up – albeit in less violent ways – recently in protesting abortion clinics. Less than before, but still shitty.

AUM SHINRIKYO

Founded in the mid-1980s as a blend of Buddhism, Hinduism, and even Christianity, this group evolved quickly into a violent cult. Much like the band, Oasis, this group was popular in the 1990s. Unlike Oasis, this doomsday cult released sarin nerve gas across five subway trains in Japan, killing 14 and injuring over 5,000. They had hoped this would start a worldwide war, but it failed, unlike the chart-topping hits of Oasis, which have been nothing short of success.

969 MOVEMENT

Yep, even Buddhism has some violent offshoots. The numbers are sacred to the attributes of Buddha, his teachings, and the virtues of Buddhist monks. This group took that and was like, fuck it, let's get involved in nationalist politics, too. They operate in Myanmar and really hate Muslims. They give white nationalists a run for their money. We are talking genocidal levels of hate, which is what has happened to the Rohingya people. The 969 movement has been particularly adept at using social media – most notably Facebook – to push false messages about the Rohingya and encourage people to support their violent activities. Thanks, Zuckerberg.

Kach and Kahane Chai

This ultra-nationalist Jewish group has a distinct honor of being labeled a terrorist organization by Israel, the US, and the EU. Their goal is to create an extremely restrictive and theocratic Israeli state – no democracy here. Their founder was assassinated in the 1990s, which only radicalized the group further (somehow). They have been responsible for massacres of Palestinians over the last several decades, hence their designation. Officially, they no longer exist. Unofficially, which is so often the case for fringe groups, they still operate in movements across the West Bank.

Sanatan Sanstha

While the Hare Krishnas represent the strange but harmless fringe of Hinduism, this group showcases the violent side of Shiva. It is relatively new, only organizing in India in 1999 as a way to safeguard Hindu culture against Muslims and Christians. This group allegedly graduated from violence to full-blown terrorism with bombings in 2008 and 2013. They have also been connected to assassinations of journalists, although they deny involvement in any violent activity. Despite these connections, they have managed to gain a large following by promoting religious and cultural programs in ashrams and temples. Sure, they may use intimidation and threats against others, but they also teach a great hot yoga class.

From the Mountaintop

Now it is time to learn about the most powerful extreme religious movements. These are the heavy hitters in terms of power and influence. These are the groups that are the top models for your dream of becoming an extremist god. They fall predominantly in the more dangerous end of the religious spectrum and deserve a bit more focus given how much influence they have compared to some of the smaller fringe groups you just learned about.

IT'S THE END OF THE WORLD AS WE HOPED IT

The Rapture. A long-held belief by Christianity that, at some point, Jesus will return and take his followers to heaven. (For those not in the know, Jesus was killed a couple thousand years ago). The rest will be left behind where they will experience great suffering, hardship, canker sores that take forever to heal, and chaos on Earth. Wait...did this shit already happen?

Figure 27: God Should Really Try Using Instagram Stories To Get This Message Out To More People.

It doesn't seem like too much of a threat anymore. The Rapture is thought to happen just before a time of trouble and chaos. There is no shortage of those times, so Jesus must be on his way, at the very least.

There is a reason that you are learning about The Rapture. There are countless religions, sects, cults, and book clubs that believe Armageddon is bound to happen soon. It is always soon. Plenty of followers are passive in regard to this 'end times' belief. They acknowledge it, maybe believe it, but don't change much in their lives except, ya know, not being a dick to everyone. That is usually enough for the gods. This is not about those followers. You aren't looking for a passive believer. There is a gold, frankincense, and myrrh mine of extremist believers if you look for it. There are a few who not only believe in the end of the world but are actively praying for it.

ONWARD CHRISTIAN SOLDIERS

Evangelical Christians can trace their roots in the United States back to the Protestant Reformation of the late 1500s. This reformation against the traditions of the church gained momentum in the 1800s through revival movements. This is where the big tents, loud preachers, and on-site conversions started to appear on Sundays. Today, tens of millions of Evangelical Christians dot churches and various denominations across the United States. Evangelicals have big followings in Latin America, too. They are particularly located in the South and Midwest, which is known as "The Bible Belt." Big, loud, and preachy sounds like 90 percent of Americans. Yet, like most religions, the majority of evangelicals are good, kind-hearted people. Hell, even Jimmy Carter was one. And he was like the nicest person ever, even after he lost that hopscotch tournament. However, there is a loud, fringe element that has managed to become more powerful over the last few decades. The subset of these bible thumpers are thumping pretty loudly in anticipation of the end days. They have become especially fervent since 1948, much to the chagrin of their moderate majority.

In 1948, Israel was formed within the historic region of Palestine in the Middle East as a haven for the Jewish people. There was a vegetarian with a drug habit who really had a grudge against them. The newly formed United Nations (another sign of the end times, world government and all that), with the help of the British and the Americans, officially declared the independence of the Israeli state. The Palestinians and the Arabs in the region approved of this plan so much that they threw the Jewish people a welcome party. They continue to have joint parties every few years up to the present day. Or is it wars? Doesn't matter.

What matters is that that this event, to these fringe evangelicals, was understood to be a fulfillment of their end-times prophecy. Several books in the Old Testament as well as the book of Revelation (the final book in the New Testament) state that the return of the Jewish people to their ancestral homeland marks the beginning of the end. Afterwards, Jesus is slated to return and

Armageddon to begin. The tension and welcoming parties between the Arabs and the Israelis have only solidified this literal translation and belief of the bible.

For these fringe evangelicals, the end of the world is a huge win. It means they get to go to heaven with all their loved ones. There is also a component of "I told you so" that they would love to throw in the face of non-believers while they burn. Thus, they cheer on the violence in the Middle East as a harbinger of the first battle between good and evil.

Father, Son, and Holy Shit

Speaking of harbingers, Donald Trump. Did you have to reread that last sentence because you thought it said hamburgers? It is OK if you did. Now that he is in his second Presidential term, Trump remains the focus of many evangelical extremists who see him as his own welcome party (different from the Arab's welcome party) to Jesus's return.

Trump does not believe in the theology of the 'end times.' To be fair, he does not believe in much of anything. He does believe in popularity and has thusly done his best to cater to the roughly 80 million evangelicals in the United States. He can be forgiven for not being able to hold a bible right side up. Reading is tough, especially without a Department of Education.

For those evangelicals who do read, they compare him to one of two people associated with the possible apocalypse.

1. Cyrus – The pagan ruler of Persia that helped the Israelites return from exile. Trump's steadfast support of Israel's settlements and moving the U.S. embassy to Jerusalem is seen as similar.

2. Jehu – An old biblical king who restored Israel and killed the worshippers who had taken it over. Again, Trump's backing of the far-right in Israel displacing Palestinians is helping to usher in the second coming.

An even more bizarre comparison believed by other evangelicals is that some of these rapture-loving evangelicals see Trump as a truly evil person. They compare him to the Antichrist who "deceives many people with his power and evil deeds before being ultimately defeated by Jesus upon his return." Thus, they tolerate him in office and his extremist policies. It is a means to a literal end.

You are probably sick of reading about white Christian nationalists. The lesson here is that embracing the Apocalypse is a surefire way to gain a few million followers to your cause who will happily accept other radical policies and ideas, as long as you herald in that bearded hippie to save them. If you can't be Christ, then why not be the Antichrist? Evil tends to pay off these days more than being a decent person.

Praise Be Upon Him

Well, this section certainly will not be controversial. Brace yourself, it is time to look at Muslim extremists. Remember when you were only learning about fake birds?

Muslim extremists are probably the most well-known of radical groups in the Western World due to their history of excessive violence, terrorism, and babka recipes. That doesn't necessarily mean that all Muslim extremists resort to flying planes into buildings. In fact, Islamic extremism got its start in the early 20th century as more of a political movement known as the Muslim Brotherhood. Pretty innocuous. Its main purpose was to establish a society governed by Islamic law and not influenced by Western government or culture. Less innocuous, but you do you.

The Iranian Revolution of 1979 and the Soviet-Afghan War the same year through 1989 fueled the push toward extremism in the Brotherhood and offshoots, including Osama Bin Laden, who did orchestrate planes into buildings. So, it is all connected.

Islamic extremism has several well-known groups that are loosely (if at all) associated with each other despite following the same ideas. Al-Qaeda is the most famous for carrying out the

9/11 attacks (or did they?). Others have had their share of violence including Boko Haram, based in Nigeria, Al-Shabaab in Somalia, or the second most famous (and most tech savvy), the Islamic State of Iraq and Syria (ISIS).

Figure 28: The Prophet Muhammad Seen Here With Harry Styles.

You may not be seeking to emulate the typical violence that is often a defining characteristic, but you should take lessons from ISIS in particular on social media recruiting and marketing. They are pretty darn good at it.

Social media excels at allowing you to push your extremist agenda as well as recruit new followers to your cause. ISIS has utilized platforms like Twitter, Facebook, Telegram, and YouTube to reach an audience around the world. Teenagers from all walks of life have left their friends and family behind to join the ISIS cause, some even dying for it. In their online videos, the group posts the benefits of joining such as a sense of belonging, adventure, purpose, and full dental and medical benefits. Plus they have a wellness program that has many more rewards than the Taliban's.

Based on a study from The George Washington University's Program on Extremism, there have been 246 separate terrorist offenses in the United States related to ISIS. 90 percent of those arrested were male. Let's face it, Islam and ISIS ain't exactly the Sisterhood of the Traveling Pants.

While many travel abroad to help ISIS fight in the Middle East, nearly 30 percent were plotting domestic terrorism in the USA. On January 1st, 2025, a 42-year-old rented a truck and drove it through the famous Bourbon street in New Orleans, Louisiana. He killed more than a dozen and injured scores more before being killed by police. He was mostly angry about not getting enough beads, forgetting that Mardi Gras was still a month away. As far as authorities know, ISIS didn't help him plan the attack, they simply got him to convert the previous summer through social media. The rest he did on his own. This is an important point, as utilizing social media can commit acts on behalf of your cause without the need to direct them. That isn't just good social media messaging, that is good delegation.

Utah Dreaming

If you have met a Mormon family, then you probably don't remember the names of all eighteen of their children. But also, they are some of the strangely nicest people on the planet. Extremism doesn't always have to be an anger-filled pustule. The Mormons' beliefs are pretty well known these days. In case you don't recall, a known grifter from the 19th century, Joseph Smith, said he found a book in Manchester, New York that was another testament of Jesus. He claimed that the Israelites were the Native Americans and migrated over to America centuries ago. A ton of people believed him and the church now has over 17 million members and basically owns the state of Utah. There is even a statute of Space Jesus there. Space Jesus!

Their massive membership also means the Church has a massive amount of funding and thus, massive influence and power. Prominent members of the Church have even held high-level political positions, like Mitt Romney. Their monetary influence has helped sway policies, and they vote in step with conservatives of the country. Plus, they really love fashion forward.

The Church remains incredibly secretive regarding both its current beliefs and, maybe more importantly, its financial practices. It is difficult to tell how much money the leaders wield and where it all goes, other than lavish temples around the world. The Mormons also have their share of child sexual abuse claims, but which religion doesn't these days? That is a feature, not a bug.

The Mormons also have a long history with polygamy, which is probably another reason why they like to keep things under wraps most of the time. This has often kept them at bit more at arm's length compared to the Christian nationalist sects in the country. One particular extremist faction of the Latter Day Saints (LDS) is the Fundamental Latter Day Saints (FLDS) who openly practice polygamy. They believe that participating in it is a divine commandment essential for achieving the highest level of exaltation in the afterlife. This also means the group participates in child marriages, sexual assault, and human trafficking. It is all OK because it is in the service of exaltation. Won't somebody think of the exaltation?

Xenu Marks the Spot

From a belief standpoint, the Church of Scientology really stretches the imagination on the origins of humanity. Not that the legacy religions are anywhere close to the truth either. This isn't about that aspect of religion though. Despite the bizarre belief system resting on an evil alien throwing people's souls into volcanoes, Scientology is no laughing matter when it comes to the power they wield. Well, you can laugh a little, especially if you like dark humor.

It was started by a science fiction writer, L. Ron Hubbard, in the early 1950s, and since his death in 1986, has been run by his successor, David Miscavige. Miscavige reigns as a god in his capacity as head of Scientology, wielding political power across the world and ruling a subservient followership at home in the United States. David and his leadership utilize intimidation and harassment to influence everyone from political leaders to freelance journalists. The author may soon join their ranks after writing this section. This intimidation tactic is known as the "Fair Game" policy that allows Scientologists to "trick, sue, or lie to or destroy anyone deemed an enemy of the church." That wasn't just a wink and a nod, that is actual policy. The Church says they no longer follow that policy, but the evidence begs to differ.

In terms of political power, the Church took on the Internal Revenue Service (IRS) and won. This 37-year-long dispute was about the right of the Church to receive tax-exempt status like the more traditional religions receive in the United States. They did this by harassing IRS officials with over 2,500 lawsuits. They committed blackmail and several other felonies to help intimidate the department into granting them tax-exempt status in 1993. They have used similar tactics on journalists, businesses, and former members.

Within the Church, brutality and slavery are routinely used and encouraged by leaders. The group's Sea Organization (Sea Org) has been accused of forced labor and human trafficking. Members are often tricked into signing 1-billion-year-long contracts and dedicate their lives to the Church. They are forced into isolation, working long hours for minimal pay. They are basically kept against their will as trying to leave is met with brutal punishment to you and/or your family. So, slaves. That's how you get slaves. It is difficult to get much more of an extreme level of follower than that. Maybe a European soccer fan, but that is it.

The Church has between 20,000 – 50,000 members in 150 organizations around the world as they have increased their presence and intimidation tactics far outside of the United States's borders. The Church shows how much power you can acquire globally while maintaining – and cultivating – your extremist ideals.

Megaphones and Megachurches

You have no doubt seen them. Massive structures dotting metropolitan centers with 5,000 seat auditoriums, modern amenities, and futuristic architecture. This is the megachurch, and it is a mega way to live out your godlike fantasies.

While the first megachurches can be traced back to the mid-19th century, they became a cultural phenomenon in the 1980s, popping up everywhere across the country. These churches draw very large congregations of loyal followers. Large congregations mean a large amount of donations, which means a large amount of influence and power. Add a hefty dose of tax exemption, stir together, and you get church leaders flying around in G5 private planes, living in massive multimillion-dollar homes, and cozying up with politicians.

Megachurches are run like multinational empires with Jesus as the Chairman of the Board. They have slick, professional television and online broadcasts run by media savvy followers. These tele-vangelists operate with a youthful energy and a businessman's tech-nique. These leaders may live like kings, but they stop one step short

Figure 29: Jesus Always Has A Sell Out Crowd

of considering themselves gods. They are rather the mouthpiece of their lord on Earth. They are basically like popes, but with more money and less linen. Similar amount of abuse though.

One of the most prominent of these "new popes" is Joel Osteen, the pastor of Lakewood Church in Houston, Texas, which boasts a congregation of 45,000 members. Their church can hold nearly 17,000 people in it and is even sponsored. It is known as the Compaq Center, which is as biblical as it sounds.

Osteen utilizes a particularly good grift at his church known as the "Prosperity Gospel" that encourages members to donate large sums to the church with promises that it will lead to wealth and success. That super convincing point has netted Osteen over $100 million including a $10.5 million mansion and a Ferrari. What is he going to do? Spread the gospel in an Acura? During Hurricane Harvey in 2017, Osteen refused to open the doors to the holy Compaq Center for shelter of victims of the disaster.

The global reach of the megachurch is impressive as most claim followers who listen to their broadcasts around the world. They have perfected the production value and the theatricality of sharing extremist views. If you are going to try and be a god, you might as well look good on TV while doing it.

The Gods Must Be Lazy

It is a tough road to becoming a god, but if you get there it has its rewards. Extremism has been pushed ever more to the forefront of politics, religion, and society. This has resulted in an increased fervor in people and their beliefs. Intense, radical ideas and emotions that were once condoned to the deepest depths of the Internet are spoken by people across all walks of life. This fervor has a snowballing effect, emboldening people to shift even further to the fringe, but even more importantly, making them utter slaves to their beliefs.

First, you get them to question, then you get them to believe, and finally you get them to believe in you.

Once it is spiritually connected, it is hard to break that belief. This is the pinnacle of extremism, and you have now reached it. But what does that mean for you now? If you are comfortably at the top, can you be considered fringe anymore? Did the destination require you to shed your extremism on the journey? Perhaps. Perhaps not. Who cares, you are in complete power now. Isn't that what this is really all about in the end? Yes.

Meander inanely...

B *I* <u>U</u>

What's the topic anyway? Who cares 💩

Waffle 21   Weakest Tangent ↓↑

 grammarVIGILANTE ✅ 4 seconds ago

Actually, if you read Thus Spoke Zarathustra like I have (six times), you'd know that free will is a myth, like Egypt. No one has ever actually "been" to Egypt, and even if they did go, they probably just looked at the pyramids and visited some city. Like Cairo, which of course is "real," (if that's what you want to believe.) Nietzsche also believed in commas, by the way. While your suffering is valid, why should I give a shit if you don't even proofraed?

 81
Degrees of Seperation from the Point

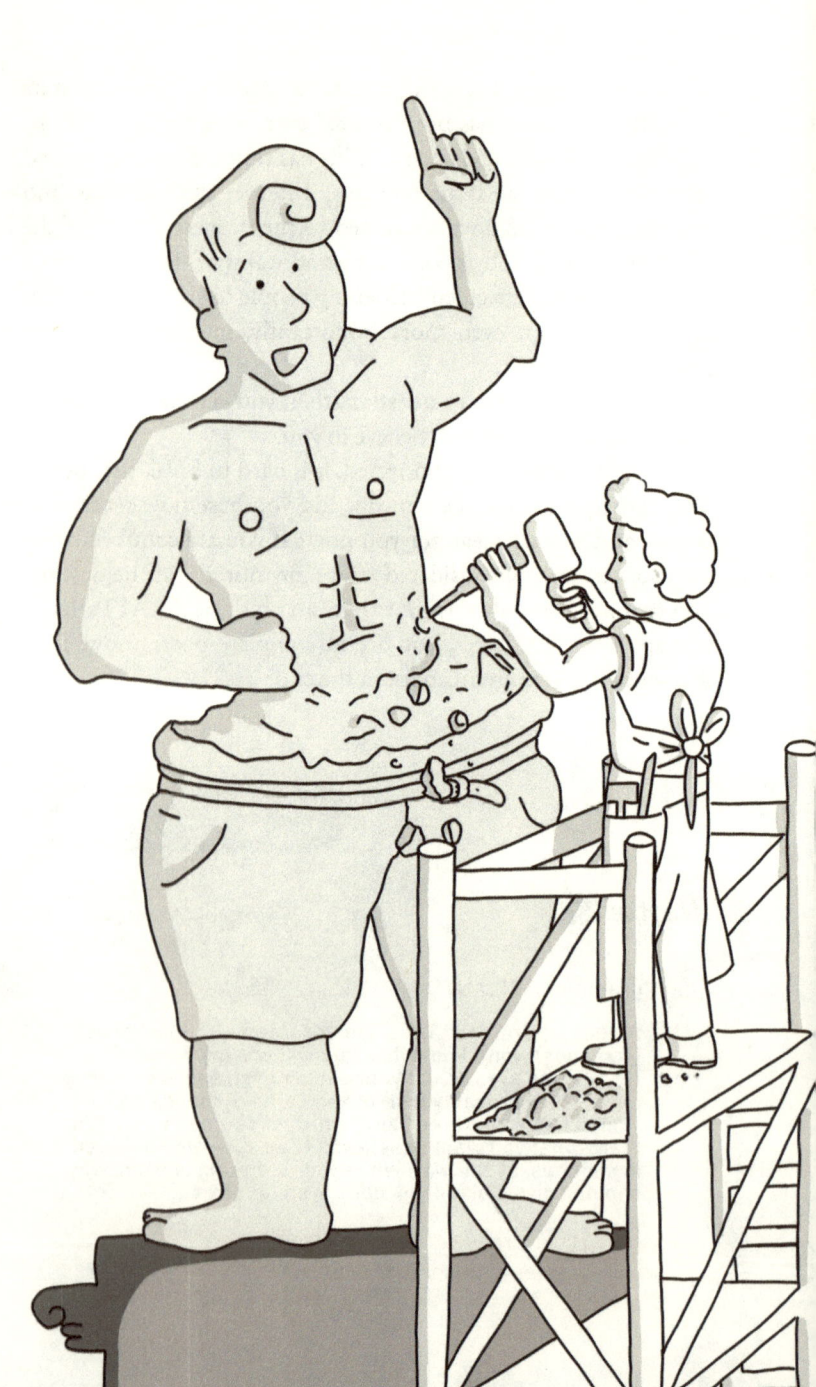

THE FINAL TRUTH

"There are no facts. Only interpretations."

— FREDERICH NIETZSCHE, GERMANY'S
LIFE-OF-THE-PARTY

Y ou have reached the ultimate truth, whatever that may be. You have reached the top of the extremist pyramid, which, like most pyramids, is encoded with predictions for Armageddon. You have discovered countless new truths that only a select few understand and cherish. You are now through the looking glass, past the curtain hiding the Great Wizard of Oz, beyond the pale, and have jumped the shark. You are the most extreme of extremists.

If you are truly smart, then you are faking it all to take what you think is rightfully yours. Because in the end, what really matters is power – whether it is from a Deep State shadow government or leading your own little cult with all its intricacies and sex parties. For it is the arbiters of truth, the heads of the movements, the religious leaders and the cult masters who are the true kings and queens of extremism. You can now count yourself among them.

You must stay vigilant, though, even at the top. For the Deep State elites and their various cronies still lurk in the shadows with their yellow, evil, beady eyes. They are waiting for you to slip up, to give up, to accept the world they have laid out for humanity. You must continue your mission to champion the truth and expose the frauds who live among us. You may not live forever – unless you really increase your servings of those supplements – but the truth will continue on after you have ascended to whatever extremist paradise you desire. Until that day, you are the guardian of it. So, hold your head up high, stick out that chest, and adjust your tinfoil hat, dear extremist.

You are the new normal now.

Appendix: The Transcendent Arbiters of Truth

There are plenty of self-proclaimed speakers of reality who have enshrined themselves into the temples of truth. The following pages list some of the most well-known – as well as some of the lesser-known examples of these great providers of facts and revelations. Never be afraid to steal characteristics, ideas, and theories from them; they would appreciate it and assume you are fighting the good fight against the blood cabals of the world. This list is non-exhaustive, but it contains the most popular extremists that grace the good flat earth we all maybe live on. These are the pioneers who paved the way, leaving in their wake pizza parlor basements, pointless rhetorical questions, braindead government officials, and most importantly, opportunities for future extremists like yourself to flourish against the dark shadow of the Bilderberg group and the Rothschilds.

STEVE BANNON

Country: Sovereign Citizen
Communication Mechanism: Podcast, Breitbart News, President Trump
Number of Followers: Permanently Banned
Cause of Extremism: Libertarianism
Interests: Alcoholism, destroying all governments, collecting commemorative stamps
Favorite Conspiracy Theory: Stop the Steal
Summary: The former chief strategist to Trump and felon (both of them) continues to be a powerful behind-the-scenes pusher of alt right theories of the Deep State, the Great Replacement Theory, and the 2020 elections. His extremist influence reaches parties in the European Union and has fueled division around the world as he yearns to bring down the world government of elites.

Nigel Farage

Country: The Post-Brexit Husk of the United Kingdom
Communication Mechanism: Legacy Media
Number of Followers: 2.1 Million
Cause of Extremism: European integration
Interests: Hating Europe, cozying up with Donald Trump, anything cold and dry
Favorite Conspiracy Theory: New World Order
Summary: This prominent British politician utilized his extremist rhetoric and beliefs, which led to Brexit. As head of the Brexit Party, he emphasized national sovereignty and Euroscepticism that often led to accusations of xenophobia and racism. Expert at tapping into public disillusionment and discontent in politics.

Guy Fieri

Country: Flavortown, USA
Communication Mechanism: Diners and Drive-Ins
Number of Followers: 2 Million
Cause of Extremism: French cuisine
Interests: Drinking Tequila with Sammy Hagar, motorcycles, leaving when Sammy gets too drunk
Favorite Conspiracy Theory: Deep Fried State
Summary: One day a porcupine had sex with a bottle of bleach and an Americana restauranter was born. His focus on food across some of America's heartland has earned him hearts, minds, and heart attacks. Fieri cultivates his followers through the Food Network with shows like *Express Lane Xtreme*, which is just one step away from inciting domestic terrorism. Probably.

MARJORIE TAYLOR GREENE

Country: United States without the blue ones
Communication Mechanism: United States House of Representatives
Number of Followers: 1.3 Million
Cause of Extremism: Needing attention
Interests: Civil war, amateur astronomy, bulking up
Favorite Conspiracy Theory: Jewish space lasers causing California wildfires
Summary: MTG represents Georgia's 14th district in Congress where she spews QAnon, anti-immigrant, and anti-LGBTQ+ rhetoric. She has excelled at preventing any useful thing from happening in government. Promotes some of the most fringe conspiracy theories about Deep State democratic child rapists and so much more. Has a big crush on Donald Trump.

TONY HAWK

Country: Skatetopia
Communication Mechanism: Half Pipe
Number of Followers: 4.3 Million
Cause of X-tremism: Getting sweet air
Interests: Spinning in one direction, spinning in the other direction, going up and down
Favorite Conspiracy Theory: Aliens invented the 900 spin
Summary: A bit suspicious as he continues to attend the X-Games despite them having extreme right in the title. The most famous and probably only skateboarder you know, Tony has since retired from skating but continues to promote X-treme products like sporting goods and Qunol's extra strength turmeric. It supports healthy inflammation responses. You should try it today!

ALEX JONES

Country: First Republic of Truth
Communication Mechanism: Rage Yelling
Number of Followers: Banned from most social media
Cause of Extremism: Skepticism of Oklahoma City Bombing
Interests: Blood pressure medication, being sued, alcoholism
Favorite Conspiracy Theory: Hormones in water turning frogs gay.
Summary: Alex has been in the conspiracy theory game since the 1990s. For decades, he used his InfoWars platform to yell against the Deep State who had control of what events happen and how they happen. Lost a $1 billion suit for claiming Sandy Hook was a false flag operation. Has since gone bankrupt.

Jim Jones

Country: Guyana, South America
Communication Mechanism: Megaphone
Number of Followers: 5,000 at peak, plus or minus 918 people
Cause of Extremism: God complex
Interests: Kool Aid, Polygamy, Slick Shades
Favorite Belief: That he will be transformed into literal incarnation of Christ.
Summary: One of the most famous cult leaders got his start at a Pentecostal, participating in "outpourings of the Holy Spirit" where you basically fall on the ground and have a seizure or speak in tongues. Surprisingly ahead of his time in promoting desegregation, which balances out his coordinated and coerced mass suicide of his followers. Take the good with the bad.

Robert Kennedy Jr

Country: Taxachusetts
Communication Mechanism: 5G Signals
Number of Followers: 4 Million
Cause of Extremism: Brain Worm
Interests: Animal carcasses, pumping iron, raw milk
Favorite Conspiracy Theory: The Plandemic
Summary: Everybody's least favorite Kennedy is the Secretary of Health and Human Services (HHS) under Trump. His beliefs in more organic, less processed food tend to be overshadowed by his extreme anti-vax stance. He was a main influence that led to a Measles outbreak in Samoa, which caused 80 deaths. Worst tropical vacation ever.

Marine Le Pen

Country: France
Communication Mechanism: Le Tweet
Number of Followers: 3 Million
Cause of Extremism: Runs in the family
Interests: Banning headscarves, anything French, hating the Muslims
Favorite Conspiracy Theory: The Great Replacement Theory (migrants replacing Europeans)
Summary: Leader of the far-right National Rally party in France that was started by her father. Very much like a French Nigel Farage, supporting Euroscepticism, anti-immigration, and populist ideals. Has run for French president multiple times and is a perpetual runner-up but remains a powerful force in France.

JENNY McCARTHY

Country: Hollyweird
Communication Mechanism: Larry King Live
Number of Followers: 1.2 Million
Cause of Extremism: Autism
Interests: Playboy magazine (just for the articles), Marky Mark's brother, bringing back measles
Favorite Belief: Vaccines Cause Autism
Summary: Former 1994 Playmate of the Year, Jenny became one of the faces of the anti-vaccine movement in 2008, voicing her opinion and deep, extensive research after her son was diagnosed with autism. Her celebrity influence boosted the movement into the mainstream. She has said if she had a choice between measles and autism, she would choose measles. Not a bad idea for a game show, maybe Jenny could host it.

AARON RODGERS

Country: Green Bay and New Jersey
Communication Mechanism: ESPN
Number of Followers: 4.5 Million
Cause of Extremism: Probably CTE
Interests: Football, Ayahuasca, Hosting Jeopardy
Favorite Belief: Anti-Vax and Deflate-gate.
Summary: Current NFL quarterback who decided to do his own research between getting tackled. In recent years, he has publicly discussed his anti-vaccine theories around COVID-19 while promoting alternative treatments like horse tranquilizer on Joe Rogan's podcast. He has also been linked to skepticism about the 9/11 attacks and the Sandy Hook shooting. Brain damage ain't no joke kids, play a different sport instead.

Joe Rogan

Country: The New United States of Rogania
Communication Mechanism: Podcast
Number of Followers: 14.1 Million
Cause of Extremism: Hosting Fear Factor
Interests: Anything unfiltered, libertarianism, Alex Jones
Favorite Belief: The Plandemic
Summary: Joe started as a standup comic in the 1980s, a gameshow host in the 1990s/2000s, and is now a sit-down joke in the 2020s. Despite this, he is one of, if not the, most powerful podcasters in the world with his reach and influence. Rogan is willing to bring anyone on to discuss all topics but has become a prime attraction for far-right voices and conspiracy theorists, giving them legitimacy. Thus, he is an extremist's best friend and megaphone.

ANDREW TATE

Country: Romania and Florida
Communication Mechanism: Twitter from Prison
Number of Followers: 10 Million
Cause of Extremism: Not loved as a child
Interests: Sex Trafficking, Sex Exploitation, Sex Assault, you name it he sexed it
Favorite Belief: Misogyny
Summary: Tate is a popular figure in the "bro far-right" and incel movements that consist of Generation Z men and boys who want to be "alpha" and troll everyone. A former kickboxer who definitely took one too many to the fivehead, Tate is in prison in Romania for sex trafficking but continues to harness a huge social media influence as well as website subscribers that nets him millions. His far-right activism includes racist, violent, and misogynistic content.

DONALD TRUMP

Country: Mar-A-Lago
Communication Mechanism: CAPITAL LETTERS
Number of Followers: 95 Million
Cause of Extremism: Barack Obama making fun of him at the White House Correspondent's Dinner
Interests: Hamburgers, Fascism, and Arnold Palmer
Favorite Belief: The Big Lie of the 2020 elections
Summary: Extremist. Felon. President. Fascist. Former McDonalds Employee. He is the total package. Although originally a Democrat, he has embraced extremist ideas for decades, targeting and reiterating conspiracy theories that involve the Deep State and elitists. He has been one of the main reasons that extremism has become normalized more than ever in the political and social sphere. Don't fret, one day he will be dead.

RON WATKINS

Country: Rural Arizona
Communication Mechanism: 8kun
Number of Followers: Unknown Millions
Cause of Extremism: Daddy Watkins
Interests: Creeping it up, cryptocurrency, being anonymous online. Those are all the same thing, really.
Favorite Belief: QAnon
Summary: One of the preeminent American conspiracy theorists that pushed the QAnon movement, which has exploded in popularity and people who ascribe to it. He was key in spreading misinformation about the 2020 election through the online website, 8kun. The website is known for white supremacy, antisemitism, and hate speech. But it also has great recipes for coffee cake.

KANYE WEST (YE)

Country: In fucking space at this point
Communication Mechanism: Bizarre clothing
Number of Followers: 30 Million (before his ban)
Cause of Extremism: Dropping out of college
Interests: Adolf Hitler, Givenchy wear, running for president
Favorite Belief: There was no Holocaust.
Summary: One of the few on this list that is banned from Twitter, which is very impressive given the state of the platform. It was only a few years ago that Ye took a far-right turn and embraced basically every antisemitic conspiracy theory on the planet and now runs in the circles of Alex Jones and Nick Fuentes (Proud Boys). He also made music, occasionally.

Actual Citations

Yes, these are actual, boring, nerd-like sources if you want to learn more without all that pesky satire. This list is far from comprehensive. If you don't care, the next page has the jokes.

1. Knight, P. (2002). *Conspiracy Nation: The Politics of Paranoia in Postwar America.*
2. Shermer, M. (2011). *Why People Believe Weird Things: Pseudoscience, Superstition and Other Confusions of Our Time.*
3. Montell, A. (2021). *Cultish: The Language of Fanaticism.*
4. Brotherton, R. (2015). *Suspicious Minds: Why We Believe Conspiracy Theories.*
5. Sagan, C., & Druyan, A. (1996). *The Demon-Haunted World: Science as a Candle in the Dark.*
6. Prooijen, J. (2018). *The Psychology of Conspiracy Theories*
7. Lantian, A., Bagneux, V., Delouvée, S., & Gauvrit, N. (2021). Maybe a free thinker but not a critical one: High conspiracy belief is associated with low critical thinking ability. *Applied Cognitive Psychology*
8. Bensley, Alan D (2023). Critical Thinking, Intelligence, and Unsubstantiated Beliefs: An Integrative Review. *National Institutes of Health, National Library of Medicine*
9. Ronson, J. (2001). *Them: Adventures with Extremists.*
10. McQuade, B. (2024). *Attack from Within: How Disinformation Is Sabotaging America.*
11. Levitsky, S., & Ziblatt, D. (2018). *How Democracies Die.*
12. Neiwert, D. (2017). *Alt-America: The Rise of the Radical Right in the Age of Trump.*
13. Alberta, T. (2023). *The Kingdom, the Power, and the Glory: American Evangelicals in an Age of Extremism.*
14. Krakauer, J. (2003). *Under the Banner of Heaven: A Story of Violent Faith.*
15. Reeve, Elle. (2024). *Black Pill: How I Witnessed the Darkest Corners of the Internet Come To Life, Poison Society, and Capture American Politics.*

RECOMMENDED READING

Kaczynski, Ted, "Industrial Society and Its Future"

Ronson, Jon, "Them: Adventures with Extremists"

West, Kanye, "Thank You and You're Welcome"

Stewart, James, "Deep State"

Hubbard, L. Ron, "The Fundamentals of Thought"

Ventura, Jesse, "American Conspiracies"

Atwood, Margaret, "The Handmaid's Tale"

Rosen, Michael, "We're Going On A Bear Hunt"

ALSO BY C.T. JACKSON

<u>Leadership Guides</u>
So You Want To Be A Dictator
So You Want To Be An Oligarch
So You Want To Be A Broligarch
So You Want To See: A Blind Person's Guide to Vision
So You Want To Be Poor: An Author's Journey

<u>Other Literary Works</u>
Slaughterhouse-Six: Slaught Harder
Between the Deep State and Me
The Girl With The Jerusalem Cross Tattoo

MEET THE AUTHOR

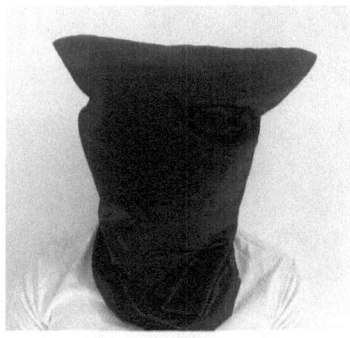

C.T. Jackson is persona non grata in fifty-seven countries, no longer allowed at the Rothschild's Villa in Southern France, and banned from most Golden Coral buffets. He has a bounty of 1.36725 Bitcoin for capture. Mr. Jackson is currently being held in an undisclosed pizza parlor's basement.

When he is not being chased by the global Deep State, he spends his time avoiding doing any real work with his wife and dog in Frankfurt, Germany.

Acknowledgments

This book wouldn't have been possible without the unquestioning support from my family, friends, and the many misinformation bots that make up the majority of the Internet.

To my wife, Melody, whose patience in spite of my radicalized rantings kept me on track. My love for her is deeper than any state.

To my mother, who taught me to check my sources and to always ask questions. This pointless, semi-cited literary work is for her.

To my fellow truthers, Alex Boeckler, Max Spitalny, and Austin Doyle who provided me with sage feedback on how to ramp up the crazy. A special thanks to Daniel Steiman, who wasted his doctorate degree on providing edits critical to the structure and integrity of the final product.

To Paul Hawkins, whose illustrations and consistent corroboration turned this book from a loon in their basement to a two-time President. He will be paid in whatever the New World Order's currency becomes.

Finally, to you, dear reader. The world has often seemed too angry, violent, and extreme. Be sure to take a minute to laugh in between it all. It can give you some perspective, maybe open up your third eye. If not, at least try a jade egg.

www.ingramcontent.com/pod-product-compliance
Lightning Source LLC
Chambersburg PA
CBHW031514120626
46545CB00005B/1871